Beginning Music Theater

The Sidewalk Labs Method

Designed for Jr/Sr High School Classroom Instruction

STUDENT NAME:

____

STUDENT WORKBOOK

2024 EDITION

A Sidewalk Labs Education Book
Student Workbook v1

All inquiries should be addressed in email to publisher@sidewalklabs.net.
www.sidewalklabs.net

ISBN: 978-1-955732-00-0

Glossary/Index

Word	Definition	Index

Repertoire Manifest

TYPE/TITLE	CHARACTER	STATUS

Section I:

Lessons

Cycle of Mastery

Phases of Experience:

Multi-Iterative Circular Routines:

Repertoire Wheel

<u>Level-Based Mastery:</u>

<u>Essentials of Level 1:</u>

Multi-Iterative Circle:

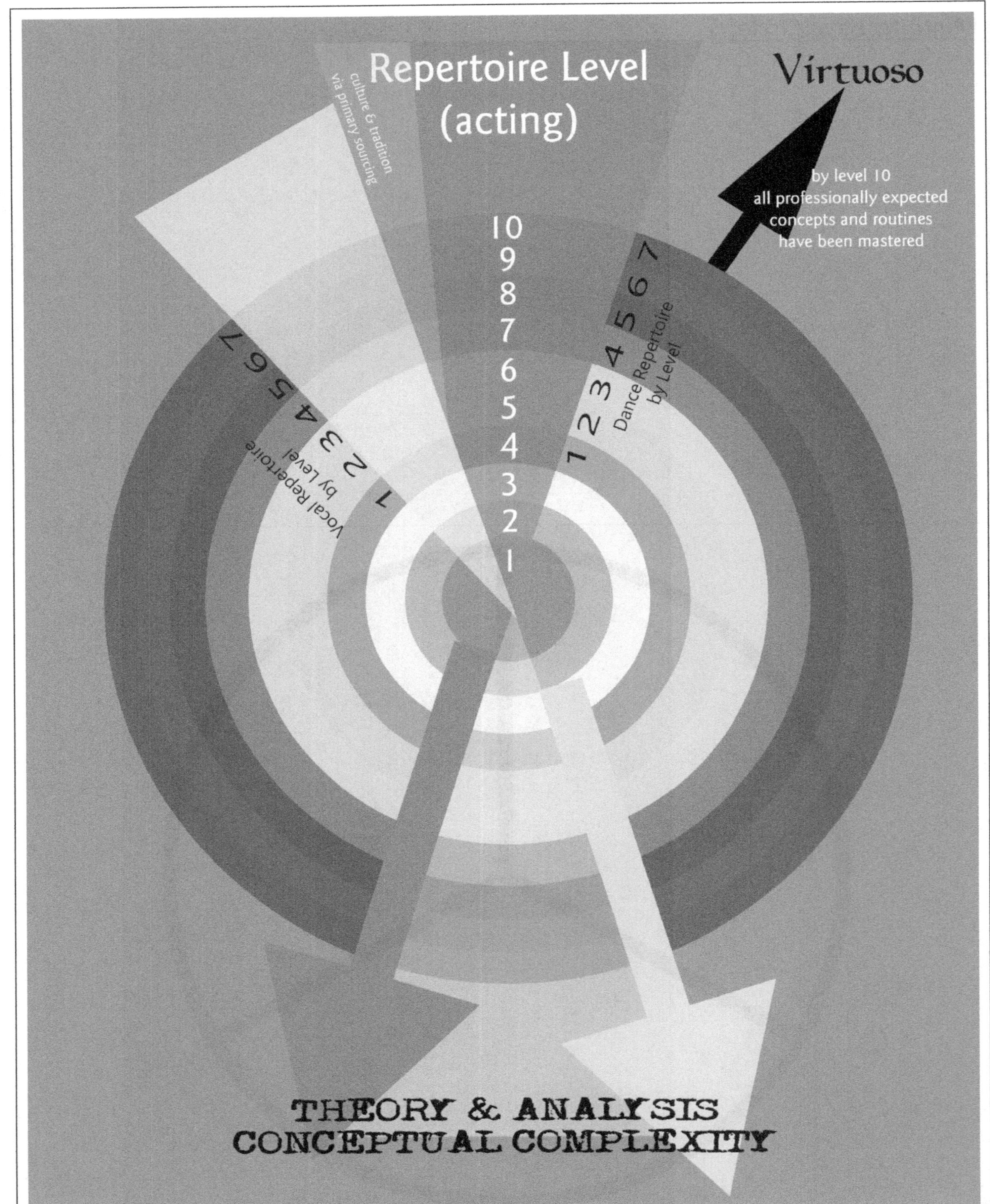
Repertoire Level
(acting)
culture & tradition
via primary sourcing
Vírtuoso
by level 10
all professionally expected
concepts and routines
have been mastered
10
9
8
7
6
5
4
3
2
1
1 2 3 4 5 6 7
Dance Repertoire
by Level
1 2 3 4 5 6 7
Vocal Repertoire
by Level
THEORY & ANALYSIS
CONCEPTUAL COMPLEXITY

Repertoire

Memorizing Repertoire:
Repertory Theater:

Monologues

Monologues in Repertoire:

Monologues as Repertoire:

Monologue Selections

Select one of the provided monologues. Analyze it using the guiding questions provided. Prepare to read it aloud in class.
Title:
Source:
Overview: Summarize the main events or ideas presented in the monologue. Identify the central theme or message conveyed by the character.
Character Analysis: Describe the character delivering the monologue. Analyze their motivations, personality traits, and background. Reflect on how these aspects shape their delivery of the monologue.

Vocabulary:

Identify any challenging ideas or concepts in the monologue. List and define any unfamiliar vocabulary encountered in the monologue.

Personal Connection:

Relate the monologue to your own experiences, emotions, or beliefs. Consider how the monologue resonates with you personally.

Monologue Readings

Take note of your impressions during the readings. Consider how you might approach each of the monologues from a performance perspective. Would you consider the monologue for inclusion in your own repertoire? Why or why not?
Performance Title:
Performance Title:
Performance Title:

Performance Title:

Performance Title:

Performance Title:

Monologues at Level 1

The Unaffected Self:
The Unaffected Concept:

Internal vs External Foundations:

Post Questions:

Why is it important to master the "unaffected self" before beginning serious work on a performance?

What does it mean for a concept to be "affected?"

Provide an example of an internal foundation other than rote memorization.

(doodle space)

Active Practice and the Unaffected Self

Active Focus:

Active Practice:

Unaffected Repertoire:

"Solitude in Public":

Post Questions:

What does "active focus" mean, and how can it benefit your performances on stage?

In the context of acting, what does it mean to present "unaffected concepts" in a monologue? Why is this important in delivering authentic performances?

What does it mean to practice "solitude in public?"

Ideas and Concepts in Theater

Theater as a Medium of Expression:

Expressing Ideas Through Characterization and Performance:

The Aesthetics of Idea:

Post Questions:

How does theater serve as a platform for social commentary? Provide an example of a play or production that effectively addressed a social issue.

How does set design play a role in presenting concepts and ideas in theater?

Imagine you are watching a play without any dialogue. How might you still be able to decode the ideas and messages being conveyed? What would you focus on?

(doodle space)

Study: Analyzing for Concepts and Ideas

Select one of the provided monologues. Analyze it using the guiding questions provided. Take one of the ideas or concepts within the monologue and prepare to describe the concept for the class. Try to be as in-depth and complete about the idea or concept as possible. Use these guided questions to help identify thoughts worth pursuing.

Title:

Source:

Key Ideas:

What are the key ideas or concepts presented in the monologue? Identify the main points the character is expressing and any underlying themes or messages.

Development of Ideas:

How does the character develop and explore these ideas throughout the monologue? Are there any shifts or progressions in their thinking or emotions?

Insights:

What insights or perspectives does the monologue offer on broader topics or issues? Consider the monologue's relevance to society, human nature, relationships, or other relevant areas of inquiry.

Inspirations:

Are there any thought-provoking or thought-provoking statements or phrases that stood out to you? What ideas presented in the monologue might you be interested in exploring more deeply?

(doodle space)

Describing Ideas

Listen carefully as each performer attempts to describe some idea or concept. Name the idea or concept for yourself. Then put it into your own words.
Idea:
Idea:
Idea:

Idea:

Idea:

Idea:

Decoding Ideas

Active Listening:
Analyzing Text:
Exploring Sub-Text:

Practical Ideas for Decoding:
Post Questions:
Other than the words themselves, what aspects of a performance can help convey ideas?
What is subtext in theater? Can you think of a situation where a character might say something but mean something different?
How does putting something into your own words help you understand its content?

Unaffected Monologue Readings

Take note of your impressions during the readings. Was the performer affected, and if so, how? Were you able to understand the ideas being presented? How unaffected was the presentation?
Performance Title:
Performance Title:
Performance Title:

Performance Title:

Performance Title:

Performance Title:

Memorized Foundation

Internal Foundation for Deeper Internalization:

Breaking Work Into Manageable Sections:

Pre-Memorization Strategies and Review Techniques:

```
H R G Q C S U V I K V M K X T W G L
F E X Y T N O S P N E O J U E T A E
G T C Q I C B L K M T C X I B I M C
N E W T N J S Y F F R E V B R X D T
I N S O L U S L U O C E R E L E N X
D T T L E X C X J U R O T N E J P E
N I E S E C T I O N S A H P A D N T
A O M R K M O W L D M L E E T L P N
T N E I C I F F E A A R L R R W F O
S U M T W K L J M T N O U L B E G C
R C O A H L D M N I J O Z T S C N I
E H R S G H Y D Q O Y T I R A L C T
D H I W L T J G J N J Z D T S I X K
N B Z S T R A T E G I E S H O V Y D
U Y A X N E L B I S S E C C A M S G
Q H B Z P E R F O R M A N C E S E M
D S L G N I N I A T R E T N E M Y R
K O E X I J P S Y S J O Q M M Z Q R
```

accessible
clarity
coherent
context
deeper
efficient

emotional
entertaining
foundation
internal
material
memorizable
performances

retention
review
sections
strategies
understanding
units

Memorizing Ideas

Decoding Ideas:
Memorizing Ideas:
Off-Page Reading:

Idea-Map:

Post Questions:

What is the first essential step when you have committed to adding a piece to your repertoire?

What should you try to avoid doing when working from a **script**?

Describe different forms an **idea map** might take.

(doodle space)

The Art of Memorization

<u>Back-to-Front:</u>

<u>Reviewing vs Repeating:</u>

Post Questions:
Name at least one reason **back-to-front** memorization may be better than **front-to-back**?
Describe the "Mount Everest Effect." Is it a motivational or demotivational effect?
Describe the "finish line effect." Is it a motivational or demotivational effect?
Why is **reviewing** more effective than **repeating**?
(doodle space)

Study: Reverse Idea Map

Choose a portion of repertoire and attempt to memorize the exact dialogue using a reverse idea map and limited review. Remember, the goal is to reach the finish line every single time, while adding more and more ideas and dialogue over time.	
<u>Reverse Idea Map:</u>	<u>Description or Reminders:</u>

Study: Idea Map

Choose a portion of repertoire and identify either large or small ideas that can be used as an internal foundation for either study or rehearsal. Create an idea map on the left of how you will organize the ideas, and jot down any helpful reminders on the right.	
Idea Map:	Description or Reminders:

Essential Elements of Theater

Theme:

Form:

Character and Characterization:

Post Questions:

How would you define the theme of a theatrical production and explain its significance in conveying messages and purposes?

Can you provide examples of different theatrical forms and explain how they influence the overall experience for both performers and audiences?

Describe how "character" and "characterization" relate to but are not the same as the characters in the play.

(doodle space)

Study: Elements in Repertoire

Consider a portion of the repertoire presented in class and consider the essential elements of theme, form, and characterization. Provide an analysis using the following study guide.
Title:
Theme: What central message or underlying idea does the play convey? How do the events in the play contribute to the exploration of the theme? What values or morals can be inferred from the characters' motivations and choices?
Form: What genre does the repertoire belong to, and how does it conform to or deviate from genre conventions? How is it structured, and how does the structure impact the storytelling? What theatrical devices are employed, and how do they enhance the audience's experience?
Character and Characterization: What are the main traits and characteristics of the central characters? How do the relationships between characters influence the plot and themes? How do the characters develop or change throughout the section or piece, and what factors contribute to their growth or downfall?

Beyond the Script

Understanding the Context:

Unpacking the Characters:

Creating Spectacle:

Post Questions:

How does understanding the historical and cultural background of a play enhance your interpretation of the story and its themes?

Describe a memorable instance of symbolism used in set design, lighting, or costumes that you believe successfully conveyed a deeper meaning in a theatrical production.

Can you provide examples of how character development and motivations drive the plot and impact the overall message of a play?

(doodle space)

Theatrical Forms

Function and Style:

Historical Trends:

Expression and Interpretation:

Post Questions:

Can you provide an example of a comedic work that effectively utilizes humor for social commentary? What makes it successful in conveying its message?

How does ancient theatre, such as Greek tragedy and Roman comedy, differ in terms of their origins, themes, and influences?

How does musical theatre combine music, dance, and storytelling to create a unique theatrical experience? Give examples of well-known musical productions and their impact.

Convergent Forms

Convergence vs Divergence:

Traditional Play Forms:

Routines:

Post Questions:
Describe the characteristics and significance of one-act plays.
Why is it important for actors and performers to understand and appreciate both convergent and divergent forms?
What are some examples of routines discussed in the lecture, apart from song and dance routines?
(doodle space)

One-Act Viewing

Themes and Messages:
What central themes are explored in the play, and how are they conveyed through the dialogue, actions, and symbols?

Setting and Stage Design:
How does the visual presentation of the set, props, and lighting enhance the storytelling and create the desired atmosphere?

Characters:
What are the motivations, conflicts, and relationships of the characters, and how are they portrayed through the actors' performances?

Directing Choices:

How do the director's choices in blocking, pacing, and emphasis contribute to the overall interpretation of the play and shape your understanding of the story?

Technical Elements:

How do the lighting, sound effects, and music enhance the production and contribute to the overall experience?

Context:

In what ways does the play relate to societal issues or historical events, and what relevance do its themes have in today's society?

Divergent Forms

Improvisational Theater:

Commedia dell'arte:

Interactive and Participatory Theater:

Site-Specific Theater:

Post Questions:

How does audience participation affect the direction and outcome of an improvisational theater performance?

How does Commedia dell'arte allow for variability in each performance despite using familiar scenarios and characters?

What is site-specific theater, and how does it differ from traditional theater performances?

(doodle space)

Divergent Throughs

Personalizing a Monologue:

Select a monologue from a theatrical play or script. Read and analyze the monologue, considering the character's background, motivations, and emotional journey.
Use micro-throughs to focus on personalizing the character's experiences and emotions, bringing your own unique perspectives to the performance. Experiment with physicality, vocal choices, and emotional nuances, exploring different interpretations and approaches. After the micro-through practice, reflect on your discoveries, noting how personalization enhanced your connection with the character and the authenticity of your performance.

Character Switch-Up:

Divide into pairs or small groups. Each participant should secretly select a character from a play or script. Without revealing their character to anyone, have participants engage in a conversation or short improvised scene while staying in character based on their chosen role. After a set period of time, talk about which characters you were representing, and switch characters. Continue the conversation or scene with the newly assumed characters. Repeat the switch multiple times, trying to fully immerse yourself in each character, considering their speech patterns, body language, and emotions.

Props and Costume Transformation:

Gather a selection of different props and costumes, such as hats, scarves, masks, or garments. Each participant chooses a prop or costume piece and uses it to transform into a unique character. Encourage participants to consider how the chosen prop or costume influences their physicality, voice, personality, and backstory. Participants should fully embody their characters and engage in improvised scenes or interactions, exploring the creative possibilities that props and costumes offer. After the activity, facilitate a discussion to reflect on the experience, sharing insights about the process of using props and costumes for character transformation in theater and the impact they have on storytelling and performance.

Instant Tableaux:

Form a group of three or four participants. Choose a moment from a scene or scenario and work together to create a frozen tableau, capturing the essence of the theme of the scene. Use bodies, facial expressions, and spatial relationships to create visually striking compositions. Find someone to observe and comment on your tableaux. After all the presentations, engage in a group discussion, reflecting on the power of visual composition and non-verbal storytelling in theater.

Forms of Practice and Rehearsal

Warm-Up Routines:

Convergent Repetitions:

Divergent Experimentation:
Convergent-Divergent Cycle
How do warm-up routines benefit actors and performers in theater practice?
Explain how repetition and consistency contribute to convergence in theater practice. Why is it important?
In what ways can divergent approaches enhance an actor's ability to interpret and portray a character?

Macro-Throughs: Rehearsal

Micro and Macro Throughs:
Purpose and Goals of a Macro-Through:
Structure and Process:
Challenges and Problem-Solving:

Micro-Throughs: Practice

Personalization:
Purpose and Goals of Micro-Throughs:
Structure and Process:
Challenges and Benefits:

Production Schedule

Stages of Production:
Fall Play:
Spring Musical:

Scenes

The History of Scenes:

The Role of Scenes:

Repertoire as Cyclical Targets:

Post Questions:

How have scenes evolved throughout the history of theater?

What are the key roles of scenes in theatrical works?

How does scene-work contribute to the development of actors?

(doodle space)

Scene Selections

Select one of the provided scenes. Analyze it using the guiding questions provided. Find a partner or partners and prepare to read it aloud in class.
Title:
Source:
<u>Overview:</u> Summarize the main events or ideas presented in the scene. Identify the central theme or message conveyed by the characters.
<u>Character Analysis:</u> Describe the characters delivering the scene. Analyze their motivations, personality traits, and background. Reflect on how these aspects shape their interactions.

Vocabulary:

Identify any challenging ideas or concepts in the scene. List and define any unfamiliar vocabulary encountered in the scene.

Personal Connection:

Relate the scene to your own experiences, emotions, or beliefs. Consider how the scene resonates with you personally. Which character do you identify with most?

Scene Readings

Take note of your impressions during performances. Consider how you might approach each of these scenes in performance, and whether you might include it in your repertoire. Who might you be able to rehearse it or perform it with?
Performance Title:
Performance Title:
Performance Title:

Performance Title:

Performance Title:

Performance Title:

Commedia Dell'arte Viewing

Plot or Message:
Can you discern the plot or scenario that is taking place? How was it presented?

Characters:
What characters appeared? Were they stock characters or more complex? How did they interact with the material and/or audience?

Improvisation:
How much was convergent, do you think? How much was made up on the spot?

Masks:
What effect do the masks have? Do they change the experience for the audience? What about the performers?

Context:
Compare and contrast commedia dell'arte to traditional theater. Do aspects of its form appear in modern dramatic performances? If so, give an example.

Plays and Musicals

The History of Plays:

Aspects of Form:

Putting Together a Musical:

Post Questions:

What are the standard aspects of the form of a play?

Explain the importance of collaboration in putting together a modern play.

Who is responsible for interpreting the playwright's vision and bringing a play to life?

(doodle space)

Read-Through Reflections, Act I

Observations: What specific details or lines of dialogue stood out to you the most during the reading, and why?
Emotional Response: How did the reading make you feel, and which character's words or actions evoked that emotion?
Interpretation: What underlying meaning or message or messages do you perceive in the reading? Consider the subtext, character dynamics, and themes presented.
Literary Elements: Choose one literary element (e.g., metaphor, symbolism, foreshadowing) present in the reading and explain how it enhances the overall impact or understanding of the performance.
Personal Connection: Did any portion of the reading resonate with any personal experiences or emotions you've encountered? If so, how did that connection influence your interpretation or appreciation of the scene?

Ideas and Concepts in Act I

Key Ideas:

What are the key ideas or concepts presented in Act I? Which ideas might be the most difficult to present or interpret with clarity in performance?

Development of Ideas:

How do the characters explore these ideas as the plot unfolds? Identify points of disagreement or friction in how characters handle or react to ideas. Are there any ideas about which all the characters are in agreement?

Insights:

What insights or perspectives does the material offer on broader topics or issues? Consider its relevance to society, human nature, relationships, and culture.

Inspirations:

Are there any thought-provoking or interesting statements or phrases that stood out to you? What ideas presented deserve the most dramatic focus in production?

Read-Through Reflections, Act II

Observations:
What specific details or lines of dialogue stood out to you the most during the reading, and why?

Emotional Response:
How did the reading make you feel, and which character's words or actions evoked that emotion?

Interpretation:
What underlying meaning or message or messages do you perceive in the reading? Consider the subtext, character dynamics, and themes presented.

Literary Elements:
Choose one literary element (e.g., metaphor, symbolism, foreshadowing) present in the reading and explain how it enhances the overall impact or understanding of the performance.

Personal Connection:
Did any portion of the reading resonate with any personal experiences or emotions you've encountered? If so, how did that connection influence your interpretation or appreciation of the scene?

Ideas and Concepts in Act II

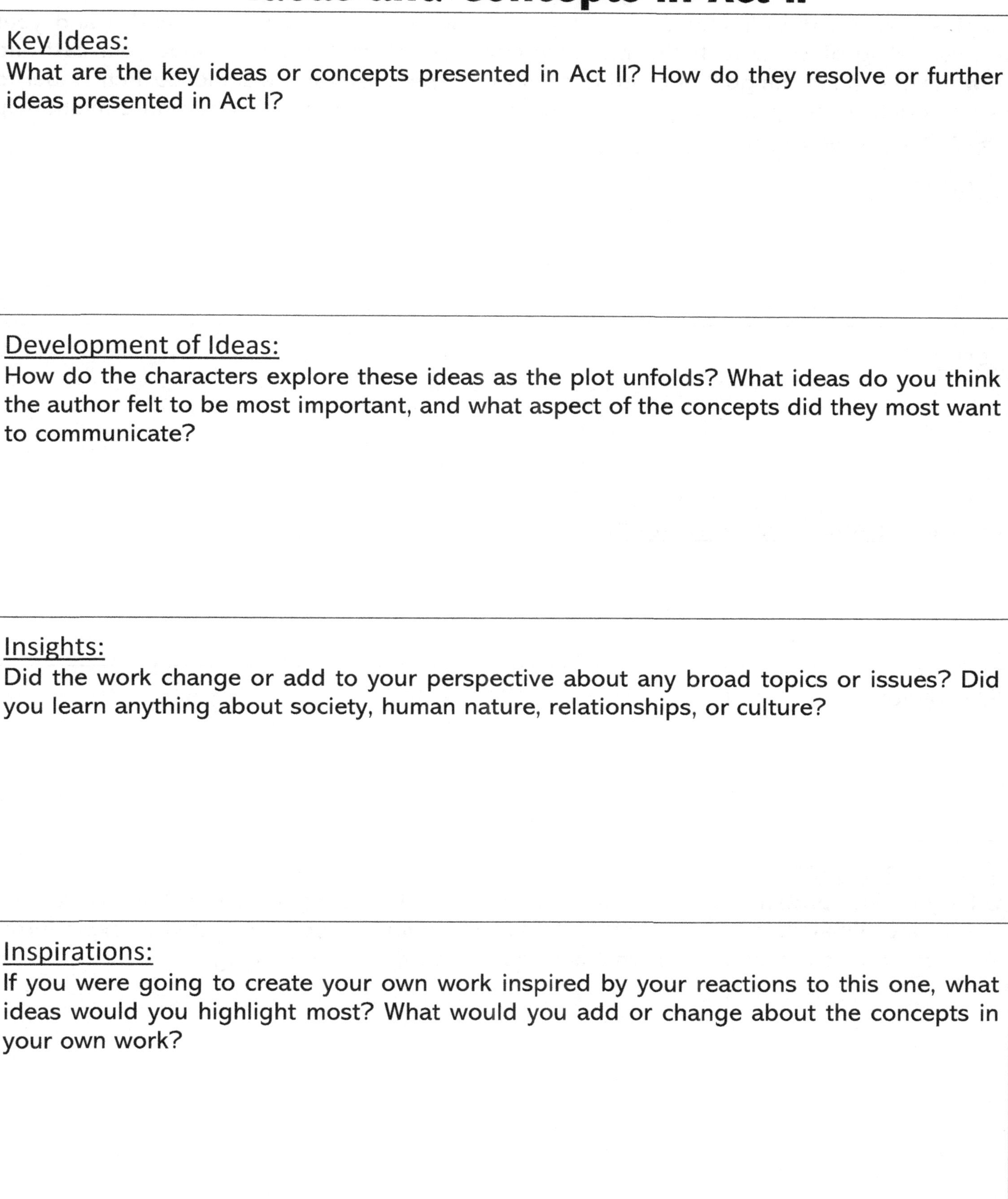

Key Ideas:

What are the key ideas or concepts presented in Act II? How do they resolve or further ideas presented in Act I?

Development of Ideas:

How do the characters explore these ideas as the plot unfolds? What ideas do you think the author felt to be most important, and what aspect of the concepts did they most want to communicate?

Insights:

Did the work change or add to your perspective about any broad topics or issues? Did you learn anything about society, human nature, relationships, or culture?

Inspirations:

If you were going to create your own work inspired by your reactions to this one, what ideas would you highlight most? What would you add or change about the concepts in your own work?

Study: Vision Statement

Imagine you are the director of the play. Use your reflections on Acts I and II and your understanding of the essential elements to craft a vision statement to guide your cast and crew. Keep in mind the goal of creating a visceral experience for the audience. Remember to include guidance for your designers and technicians on what dramatic techniques might help best achieve your vision.

Theme:
Form:
Characters and Characterization:
Spectacle:
Vision Statement: Offer your interpretation and opinion of the material, including any aspect that you found interesting. What do you like about it? What elements are you interested in exploring? What do you dislike about it or what aspects do you find uninteresting?

Purposeful Affectation

Purposeful Active Practice:

Idealized Affectations:

Internalizing and Naturalizing Affectations:

Projecting the Voice:

Post Questions:

Explain the concept of idealized affectations and give an example of how incorporating an affectation can enhance a character's portrayal.

How does affecting volume, specifically projection, contribute to a more impactful and engaging performance on stage?

Name the muscle that is responsible for breath support.

Layering a Performance

Performance Depth:

Theory Layers (Study):

Technique Layers (Practice):

Active Practice: the Method

Method:
Result 1:
Result 2:

Result 3:
Draw a graph of the boredom effect. Then, draw on top of it a graph of your own boredom effect as you see it in relation to the "average."
How many targets should you have at one time?
How do you know if you've succeeded in active practice?
(doodle space)

Leveling Standards

Leveling Skills:

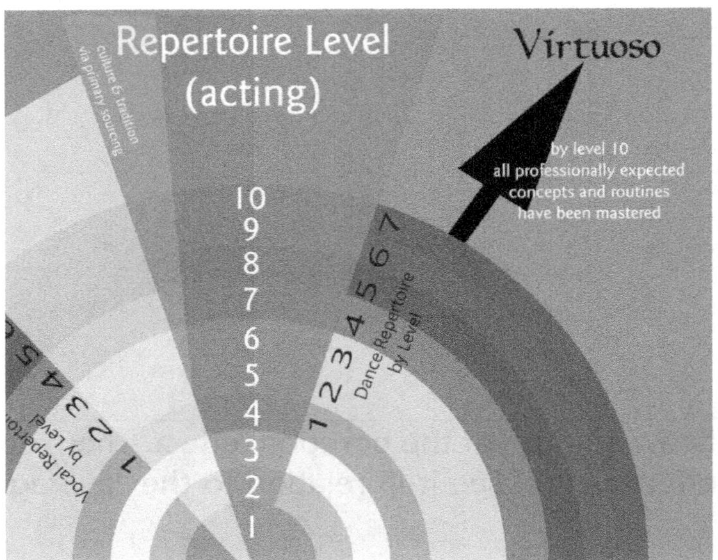

Leveling Repertoire:

Level 1 Minimums:

Level 2 Minimums:

Level 3 Minimums:

Beyond Level 3:

Monologue Leveling Chart

Name of Monologue: (if it has no official title, use the first phrase or sentence and the name of the show)	
Source of Monologue: (ideally the name of the full show from which it was taken and the writer or creator)	
Elements of Complexity:	
Length	
Vocabulary	
Setting	
Stage Directions	
State-of-Being	
Character	
Other Considerations	
Estimated Level:	

Activity: Three Changes Over Ten Rounds

Work on a portion of a monologue or a scene by running it through active practices. Perform the section at least ten times in a row, interrupting repetitions only to change active focuses. Change active focuses at least three times and journal the outcomes.
Title:
Focus 1:
Focus 2:
Focus 3:
Focus 4:
Title:
Focus 1:
Focus 2:
Focus 3:
Focus 4:

Level 2A: States of Being

Identifying States of Being:
Simple and Complex States of Being:
Naming States of Being:
What two things should an effective name of a state of being include?
Name one state that you've experienced enough you believe you could easily draw on it as an actor.

Processing States of Being

Experiencing:
Remembering:
Expressing:
What two things should an effective name of a state of being include?
Name one state that you've experienced enough you believe you could easily draw on it as an actor.

Inhabiting States of Being

Naturally Affected States:

Experiencing Naturally Affected States:

Re-Inhabiting a Previous State:

Study: State of Being Layer

Choose a piece of repertoire. List scenes, sections, or lines, and next to those, try to name the state of being experienced by the character at that time. Remember characters are *always* experiencing some state.

Section:	State of Being:

Dynamics in States of Being

Modulating Intensity:

Dynamics in Voice, Tone and Pace:

Practicing Dynamic Range:

Post Questions:

Why is it important to vary tone and pace in dialogue delivery?

How does this contribute to the overall dynamics of a scene?

Describe the relationship between dynamics and dramatic shape.

(doodle space)

Affected Monologues: State of Being

Take note of your impressions during the performances. Can you identify what state the character is in? Does the actor seem more affected by the character's state or their own?
Performance Title:
Performance Title:
Performance Title:
Performance Title:

Performance Title:

Performance Title:

Level 2B: Maintaining a Target

<u>Attention:</u>

<u>Spotlight of Attention:</u>

<u>Responsive Targets:</u>

Unless otherwise directed by stage directions, where should you practice keeping your attention at level 2?
What is meant by a responsive target, and how might trying to focus on one change a performance?

```
R O H P A T E M T O Z V X V G H F D D P R
J V N Y N S N R G I R E I T N R I R E S E
S L B G B U Q B A Q F O C U S Y G P P T S
T N E M E G A G N E E R N D I T H O T O P
K P E Y X G V N K Y E B I B X I T B H Y O
X R U Z L N P Q C T D T U I C L A W T A N
R E L G B Y C Y C E G E P O I I E E Y X S
B S L Y Y D W A T A C V V G E B O D Y Q I
W E H Z I D R L N I M P H B N A S G C H V
J N D H D A Y I O K C T H O E T S J Z J E
W T M P H I M A N R E I T F C P Z R Q D P
L X O C R A S O A C T M T J S A D W F X X
J K N W T A I T N D L N B N Y D K J V Y V
Q H S E I T C A R I P C O Y E A Q P Z F N
A R Z O N L M T N A U B G C O H E B L A P
J N I E R R X T I S C O B J E C T I V E S
Z L T F O P E Z D C K T R R A Y H U Q V E
N T L F R R F D T G E D I A U D O U A W E
A Q R G A N B C C U X F A O Z O D S E J B
R E U C X T B G Q T U X N F N T A R G E T
P C T B E G K I I A J G E Y W S Z I U B J
```

adaptability	distractions	performance
animate	engagement	practice
attention	focus	present
authenticity	interact	responsive
character	metaphor	scene
control	nuance	spotlight
depth	objectives	target

Circles of Awareness

Spotlight Metaphor:
Area:
Focus:
Intensity:

Activity: Mental Spotlight

Work on a monologue or a scene by running it through several repetitions. Each time, make an adjustment to some aspect of your spotlight of attention: target, area, focus, or intensity. Only adjust one element at a time and record your impressions of how it affected you or the performance.
Title:
Spotlight:
Impressions:
Title:
Spotlight:
Impressions:
Title:
Spotlight:
Impressions:

Affected Monologues: State of Being/Targets

Take note of your impressions during the performances. Can you identify what state the character is in or what their attention is focused on? Does the actor seem more affected by the character's state or their own? How focused or effective is their attention?
Performance Title:
Performance Title:
Performance Title:

Performance Title:

Performance Title:

Performance Title:

Acting vs Pretending

Acting as Surface Presentation:

Pretending as Imagined Experience:

Combining Acting and Pretending:

Level 2 Monologues

Take note of your impressions during the performances. Can you identify what state the character is in or what their attention is focused on? Does the actor seem more affected by the character's state or their own? How focused or effective is their attention?
Performance Title:
Performance Title:
Performance Title:

Performance Title:

Performance Title:

Performance Title:

Auditioning with Monologues

Developing Repertoire for Auditions:

Choosing Monologues That Fit You:

Adding Depth to Performance:

Tailoring Monologues to Auditions:

Post Questions:

Why is it important for actors to have a variety of monologues in their repertoire for auditions?

Why is it essential to be flexible with your monologue choices and tailor them to fit specific audition requirements?

Can you give an example of how understanding the background and motivations of a character can enhance your monologue performance?

List below a few monologues that you think might fit both you and potential audition situations.

Mock Auditions

As you view mock audition song presentations, imagine you are a part of the casting team. Use the following rubrics to help guide your critique of their audition.

Performer:		
Vocal Projection	1 2 3 4 5	**Notes:**
Pitch/Intonation	1 2 3 4 5	**Notes:**
Breath Control	1 2 3 4 5	**Notes:**
Range	1 2 3 4 5	**Notes:**
Expressiveness	1 2 3 4 5	**Notes:**
Positives:		**Negatives:**

Performer:		
Vocal Projection	1 2 3 4 5	**Notes:**
Pitch/Intonation	1 2 3 4 5	**Notes:**
Breath Control	1 2 3 4 5	**Notes:**
Range	1 2 3 4 5	**Notes:**
Expressiveness	1 2 3 4 5	**Notes:**
Positives:		**Negatives:**

Performer:		
Vocal Projection	1 2 3 4 5	**Notes:**
Pitch/Intonation	1 2 3 4 5	**Notes:**
Breath Control	1 2 3 4 5	**Notes:**
Range	1 2 3 4 5	**Notes:**
Expressiveness	1 2 3 4 5	**Notes:**
Positives:		**Negatives:**

Performer:		
Vocal Projection	1 2 3 4 5	**Notes:**
Pitch/Intonation	1 2 3 4 5	**Notes:**
Breath Control	1 2 3 4 5	**Notes:**
Range	1 2 3 4 5	**Notes:**
Expressiveness	1 2 3 4 5	**Notes:**
Positives:		**Negatives:**

(notes)

Auditioning with Song and Dance

Selecting a Piece:
Bringing Emotion into Song:
Vocal Technique:

Understanding a Dance Audition:

List below a few songs that you think might fit your voice and be usable in a real audition situation.

(notes)

Mock Auditions

As you view mock audition monologue presentations, imagine you are a part of the casting team. Use the following rubrics to help guide your thoughts. Imagine the performer is auditioning for a particular role. What did they show that made you believe they could pull it off? What did you need to see that you didn't?

Performer:

Spoken Diction/Projection	1 2 3 4 5	**Notes:**
Stage Presence	1 2 3 4 5	**Notes:**
Concentration	1 2 3 4 5	**Notes:**
Authenticity	1 2 3 4 5	**Notes:**
Character	1 2 3 4 5	**Notes:**

Positives:	**Negatives:**

Performer:

Spoken Diction/Projection	1 2 3 4 5	**Notes:**
Stage Presence	1 2 3 4 5	**Notes:**
Concentration	1 2 3 4 5	**Notes:**
Authenticity	1 2 3 4 5	**Notes:**
Character	1 2 3 4 5	**Notes:**

Positives:	**Negatives:**

Performer:

Spoken Diction/Projection	1 2 3 4 5	**Notes:**
Stage Presence	1 2 3 4 5	**Notes:**
Concentration	1 2 3 4 5	**Notes:**
Authenticity	1 2 3 4 5	**Notes:**
Character	1 2 3 4 5	**Notes:**

Positives:	**Negatives:**

Performer:

Spoken Diction/Projection	1 2 3 4 5	**Notes:**
Stage Presence	1 2 3 4 5	**Notes:**
Concentration	1 2 3 4 5	**Notes:**
Authenticity	1 2 3 4 5	**Notes:**
Character	1 2 3 4 5	**Notes:**

Positives:	**Negatives:**

(notes)

Inhabiting the Moment

The Art of Inhabiting:

Inhabiting a Character:

Inhabiting a Sequence:

What is the meaning of **sequence** in the context of theater?
Provide one method you might use to better **inhabit** a character or sequence?
How might one prepare to **inhabit** a character?

R E O Z G E P C R T J L N A L P C P E P Z T
H E U S G M F E N Y U T U D S R O W M N I R
S F T U E A R E B B P T G N S E V A L R V N
I F Z C W Q M W W T H Y Z I B S Y I I M V E
L F D C A O U E B E H D V M E E I P Z N C V
B A K U M R I E N I X R T P X N S B J W V I
M Q C S O M A T N S I M C S P C F J O C T S
O K D T R K I H O C Y X E T A E N G A G E R
Y S W O O C D L C A E C N A M R O F R E P E
S Y J I I R G U R R T S H G V A F P I B G M
S Y H T N W K T D B T J O E S O P R U P H M
N G Y U I V R Q Q X E X X B H O R U N F R I
R A T H A O R O U T I N E F W B C R Y G V C
O A R G P B G J N L K A O V O O L B H D Q Y
A R X H I C D K O P V B X I N I P M G Q T A
R W S C O A S U I Y N C D N T H E A T E R B
U N D U Q L F M T M T G E E S I N C P E C C
I C F B R P U Q O Y O C H R Q D S P U T Z K
Z S V Q U D E B M Y T Y O I T I A N A O Z G
P N H L U Q Q T E I D Y X R V N O K A W R T
J P X G Z M L W O T W O T P C F H N Z R B F
A Y O B P U M N L I J T B N O S T Y U E T X

actor
authenticity
body
character
connection
emotion
engage
immersive
mind
moment
performance
portray
presence
purpose
routine
sequence
spirit
stage
theater
transition

Experiencing Through Pretend

Vicarious Experience:
Role-Play Outside of Theater:
Communion Through Pretend:

Communion

Stanislavski:
Personal Resources:

Achieving Communion:
Authentic Communion:
According to Stanislavski, what should an actor share with other actors at every moment on stage?
Finish this quote: "The vacant eye is…"
What does it mean to have achieved communion on stage?

Communion with a Target

Exchange of Resources:

Communication and Communion:

Attention and Targets:

Study: Identifying Targets

Choose a character. Identify moments or events where your character is clearly in communion with someone or something. Identify what resources the character is trying to give or receive, and how they are trying to achieve that. Why does the communion end? What target arises to replace it?

Scene/Character:	
Event or Interaction	Target, Resources Exchanged

Theater for Personal Growth

Growing Personal Resources:

Mastering Habits and Characteristics:

Managing Internal States:

Personal Theater

Inner Theater:

Outer Theater:

Physical Theater:

Post Questions:

How are **inner theater** and **outer theater** related?

Explain why your **personal theater** can't be fully understood by someone else?

Give an example of **physical theater**.

(doodle space)

Personal Resources

Importance of You:

Resources of Character:

Meaningful Expression:

Post Questions:

What is the lifelong job of a performing artist?

Give an example of a personal resource that you have in abundance. How might you use it in the creative arts?

What makes expression *meaningful* instead of just *personal*?

(doodle space)

Study: Understanding the Self

How I See Myself:	How I Think Others See Me:
Memories of Value:	Meaning:
What are some of your most vivid and important memories? Be only as detailed as you are comfortable with, but enough that you can identify the memory with clarity.	How might aspects or impressions of this memory be meaningful to someone else? What would you want someone else to learn from it?
I Care Most in Life About:	
Most Proud Of:	Biggest Regret:
I Asked Someone About Me and They Said:	

<table>
<tr><td colspan="3"><u>Inspirations:</u>
What are your favorite things? Activities, artists, songs, movies, people, things, etc... What qualities about these things do you enjoy or admire?</td></tr>
<tr><td colspan="3"><u>In 5 Years, I Hope:</u></td></tr>
<tr><td colspan="3"><u>In 10 Years, I Hope:</u></td></tr>
<tr><td colspan="3"><u>By the End of My Life, I Hope:</u></td></tr>
<tr><td colspan="3"><u>If I Were a Creative Artist:</u></td></tr>
<tr><td>I would work in the field of:</td><td>I would create in the style or genre of:</td><td>My works would focus on the subject of:</td></tr>
</table>

Inner and Outer Experience

Internalization vs Manifestation:

Subjective vs Objective Experience:

Mental Modeling:

Post Questions:

What is the purpose of creating a **mental model**?

How is **subjective experience** an important part of theater?

Describe what is meant by **manifestation**.

(doodle space)

Study: Inner Studio

<table>
<tr><td colspan="2">Look into your mind for the objects that move through it. What types of objects dominate your thoughts? What characterizes your inner theater already when you don't try to control it? Give your thinking style a unique name and describe it briefly below.</td></tr>
<tr><td colspan="2"><u>Thinking Style:</u></td></tr>
<tr><td>Examine this list of inner theater types. How much do you automatically use each of these? Use 10 as a maximum and 1 as a minimum.</td><td rowspan="9">What are some mental objects (memories, ideas, and any verbal, visual, auditory, spatial, kinesthetic, social or emotional content) that mean the most to you? Identify at least 3 or 4 meaningful objects that could be used for resonant inner theater.</td></tr>
<tr><td>Verbal (words):</td></tr>
<tr><td>Visual (images):</td></tr>
<tr><td>Auditory (sounds or music):</td></tr>
<tr><td>Spatial (locations or shapes):</td></tr>
<tr><td>Mathematical (logic or numbers):</td></tr>
<tr><td>Kinesthetic (physical sensation):</td></tr>
<tr><td>Social (people and relationships):</td></tr>
<tr><td>Emotional (feelings):</td></tr>
<tr><td colspan="2">What is your favorite subject?</td></tr>
<tr><td colspan="2">What do you think about most? Is there a type of inner theater you use that isn't listed?</td></tr>
<tr><td colspan="2">How often do you share your inner thoughts with others? How do you feel about sharing your inner thoughts?</td></tr>
</table>

Activity: Some Kind of Interview

Prepare a list of questions you might ask someone to find out more about them. Then choose a character, and think about how you might answer those questions from their perspective. Then, observe the improvised interviews based on these reflections, and record your impressions.
Questions:
Answers:
Interview Impressions:

Interview Impressions:

Interview Impressions:

Interview Impressions:

Extending the Self

Being Present:
Being Malleable:

Growing in Character:

Post Questions:

How do you think growing as a person through life experiences can help you represent authentic characters in your acting?

Can you provide an example or a situation where this might apply?

Can you explain what it means to "be present" as an actor, and why is it important in both acting and everyday life?

(doodle space)

Soliloquy

History of Soliloquy:
Character Development:
Performing a Soliloquy:

Communion with Self

Inner Communion:
The Head:
The Heart:
The Stomach and Feet:

Guided Study: Substitution

Scene and Character:		
Idea or Concept:	**Resonant Circumstance:**	**Inner Theater:**

Study: Substitution

Scene and Character:		
Idea or Concept:	Resonant Circumstance:	Inner Theater:

Idea or Concept:	Resonant Circumstance:	Inner Theater:

Level 3: Layering Circumstances

Given Circumstances:
Dialogue and Script:
Stage Directions:

Given Circumstances

Importance of Given Circumstances:
Analyzing Given Circumstances:
Applying Circumstances:

Implied Layers

Implied Circumstances:
Analysis Layers:
Play Level Layers:

Character Level Layers:

Identify given circumstances from the play, and use those to identify two or three other things that are implied by that given circumstance.

Given:	Implied:
Given:	Implied:
Given:	Implied:

(doodle space)

Deepening Circumstances

Implied Circumstances:

Imagined Circumstances:

Layering Circumstances:

Post Questions:

Consider a given circumstance from a particular work. Use that circumstance to come up with two more implied circumstances.

How are implied and imagined circumstances related to background layers of a performance?

Describe how an imagined circumstance might completely change an interpretation of a scene. Use specific examples.

(doodle space)

Background Layers

Backstory:

Subtext:

Connecting to Backstory and Subtext:

Post Questions:

What is the difference between backstory and subtext?

Give an example of backstory from your monologue or scene.

Give an example of subtext from your monologue or scene.

(doodle space)

Analysis Layers

Given Layers:

Historical and Cultural Layers:

Performance Layers:
Post Questions:
How does the historical setting of the musical influence its themes and character portrayals?
Give one example each of a given layer, a historical or cultural layer, and a performance layer.
How does the understanding the author's background affect the interpretation of a work?
(doodle space)

Level 4: Developing a Character

Circumstances:

Motivations:

Characteristics:

Post Questions:

Give an example of a circumstance that might define a character.

Give an example of a motivation that might influence a character.

Give an example of a characteristic.

(doodle space)

Methods of Acting

Formal Systems:

Minimalist Approaches:

Physical Theater and Mime:

Minimalist Acting

Minimalist vs Method:
Embracing Your Authentic Self:
Stillness and Silence:

Physicality and Movement:
How does minimalist acting differ from other acting styles?
Can you think of any famous actors known for their minimalist acting approach? How have they influenced the industry?
What is the first step to minimalist character creation?
(doodle space)

Minimalist Viewing

Character:
What aspects of the acting changed as the actor changed characters? What stayed the same?

Stillness:
How did the actor use stillness or silence to express emotions or ideas? Give specific examples, if you saw any.

Movement:
How did the actor use movement to enhance the performance? How did their handling of movement change between characters?

Context:
Compare and contrast the effect of minimalist acting compared to other acting styles. What are its advantages and disadvantages?

Methods of Character Building

Building Character Through Desire (Motivation):

Building Character Through Manifested Traits (Characteristics):

Building Character Through Circumstances (Backstory):

Layering Characteristics

Building Character Through Manifested Traits (Characteristics):
Internalizing Characteristics:
Sublimation to the Subconscious:

Study: 3-Dimensional Character

Choose a character (or two) and identify or make up aspects from each of the given dimensions. Categorize each aspect as a **motivation**, a **characteristic**, or **backstory**.

Character:

Motivations:	Characteristics:	Backstory:

Character:

Motivations:	Characteristics:	Backstory:

Study: Pretending to Be a Character

Imagine that instead of being yourself, you actually *were* one of the characters in your repertoire. Imagine living your life as that character. How would it change your relationship with your friends, your family, or your peers? Pick a specific part of your day or your life and role-play it as the character. What would be better about actually being that character instead of yourself? What would be worse?

Character:

Life Scenario	Good Stuff	Bad Stuff	Neutral Stuff

Character:

Life Scenario	Good Stuff	Bad Stuff	Neutral Stuff

Character:

Life Scenario	Good Stuff	Bad Stuff	Neutral Stuff

Study: Staying in Character

Choose a character. Identify a few characteristics that help identify that character, then try to stay "in character" through the remainder of the class. To help, jot down active techniques or focuses that help you maintain the character state. Afterwards, jot down what made it difficult or caused you to break out of character.

Character:

Characteristics	Techniques	Active Focuses

Post Reflections:

Character Performances

Consider how each performer portrays the character. What methods do you think they might have used? How did the method affect the performance?
Performance Title:
Performance Title:
Performance Title:

Acting a Sequence

Dialogue and Stage Directions:
Communion Skills
Characterization Skills:

Study: Act I (Form)

Overview:

Summarize the plot and overall narrative arc. Identify its most dramatic moments and how they fit within the scope of the whole.

Scene Analysis:

Identify the individual scenes. How are they labeled? Clarify how the setting has changed for each scene.

Study: Act II (Form)

Overview:

Summarize the plot and overall narrative arc. Identify its most dramatic moments and how they fit within the scope of the whole.

Scene Analysis:

Identify the individual scenes. How are they labeled? Clarify how the setting has changed for each scene.

Study: Listen Through Reflections, Act I

Observations:
How did listening to the songs impact your view of the musical as a whole?

Style and Tradition:
Describe the music. What style, genre, or traditions does it seem to be drawing from?

Set-Pieces or Standouts:
Do any of the pieces seem particularly large, significant, or impactful? What aspect of the piece creates this effect? Why is it intended to stand out?

Personal Connection:
How do you personally respond to the addition of the music? What do you like or dislike about it? Any favorite pieces?

Study: Listen Through Reflections, Act II

Observations:

How did the addition of music to the play change its outcome or effect? Did it alter your ideas of theme, character, or other essential elements?

Style and Tradition:

Did the style change between Acts I and II?

Set-Pieces or Standouts:

Do any of the pieces in this act seem particularly large, significant, or impactful? Why do you think they were placed where they were in the overall form?

Personal Connection:

How do you personally respond to the addition of the music? What do you like or dislike about it? Any favorite pieces?

Voice and Song

Projection and Register Review:
Breath Support:
Pitch Control:
Acting and Singing:

Voice and Register

Projection Review:
Independent Control:
Phonation and the Vocal Folds:
Vocal Register:
Post Questions:
How is **vocal register** different from **volume**?
How is **speaking range** related to **singing range**?
When you change your **volume**, what should you be careful *not* to change?

Register-Adjusted Monologues

Take note of your impressions during the performances. How does the change of register impact the performance? How natural is the performer's use of the adjusted register?
Performance Title:
Performance Title:
Performance Title:

Performance Title:

Performance Title:

Performance Title:

Reading Music By Shape

Basic Ideas of Pitch and Duration:

Shapes on a Staff:

Uniting Eye and Ear:

Sing Through, Act I

Scene Title or Description:
Rehearsal Focus:
Intentions:
Results and Considerations:

Sing Through, Act II

Scene Title or Description:
Rehearsal Focus:
Intentions:
Results and Considerations:

Level 5: Creating a Performance Sequence

Interpreting a Script:
Discovering True Character:

Diagramming and Rehearsing:

Post Questions:

What are the key components of a musical theater performance?

Give an example of a diagram that might be useful in developing a final performance sequence.

How does interpreting a script relate to discovering the true character of a scene?

(doodle space)

Aesthetic Analysis

Aesthetics:

Aesthetic Design:

Aesthetic Analysis:

Dramatic Shape

Elements of Dramatic Shape:

Three-Act Structure:

Plotting Dramatic Shape:

Post Questions:

How does the initiating action in a musical set the tone for the entire performance?

Can you identify a musical that deviates from the traditional three-act structure? How does it impact the storytelling?

Discuss how the resolution phase contributes to the overall satisfaction of a musical theater experience.

(doodle space)

Tight and Loose Sequences

Studying a Sequence Through a Multi-Iterative Cycle:
Tight Sequences vs Loose Sequences:
Orchestrating a Moment:

Sequencing in Layers

Complexity Through Layering:

Active Practice and Individual Elements:

Sublimation and Integration:

Post Questions:

What does the term "sublimation" refer to in the context of practicing music theater, and how does it affect a performer's final presentation?

Describe briefly what is meant by **active practice**.

What are a few of the most important layers to practice in the early development of a character?

(doodle space)

Sequencing Targets

Emotional Rhythm (Beats):
Establishing Gravity:

Weaving the Inner and the Outer:

M V X E O P S I P T J O N P R X H N F
O K N V K Y V H F Y W O Z E C Q B Q K
T S W U X G Y B R B I L X Y B R Z R F
I V I A O S F D K T Q A E E J D A W Z
V K J N I Y R F A T J I Z C T T A A S
A E H C T G L Z W S X T H O M V A G B
T T A B O E I F N V O A M N G C N N Y
I L S M S L R H R J X P H T E K H I E
O J V L A U Z A S O X S G A E J F H F
N G U C U X C I C H A R A C T E R T F
Z S O B S N J O R T S M O T P D L A F
P V T I Y C E Z F P I R G O P J X E D
M M O E Q W G M A E D O S M M H V R I
M G L Y N R J V E A M T N E G G C B Q
X O X H S F R D C X U O R T E L W Z K
S E R U T S E G W R M O T P F C U U S
A W W J B N X B E V U Q L I D R Z K V
U E W Q A K E X P R E S S I O N J G A
N O I T A S I V O R P M I M V N B S Z

arc	eye contact	motivation
breathing	focus	physical
character	gestures	posture
emotion	improvisation	spatial
expression	interaction	vocalization

Scene Objectives

Understanding Scene Objectives:

Character Development Through Objectives:

Executing Objectives in Performance:

Post Questions:

How does a scene objective relate to a character in a scene?

How might the director determine the overall scene objective?

Give an example of a scene objective using a specific scene.

(doodle space)

Character Objectives

Scene Objectives vs Character Objectives:

Types of Character Objectives:

Applying Objectives in Performance:

Post Questions:

How are character objectives different from scene objectives?

Describe a super-objective and provide an example from an actual piece of repertoire.

Why is it important for an actor to maintain consistency in portraying their character's objectives throughout a performance?

(doodle space)

Through-Lines and Life Circles

Characters and Goals:
Characters and Habits:

The Passage of Time:

Post Questions:

Choose a character from a well-known musical. What is their primary through-line, and how does it influence their actions throughout the story?

Identify a recurring habit or routine of a character in a musical you have studied. What characteristic or personality trait did this reveal?

How might the through-lines of two different characters in the same play intersect or conflict with each other

(doodle space)

Study: Character Objectives

Choose a character. Identify the character's objectives in each scene, and whether they are achieved or thwarted. How do the results of each objective lead to the next?

Character Notes:	Scene 1:
	Scene 2:
	Scene 3:
	Scene 4:
	Scene 5:
	Scene 6:
	Scene 7:
	Scene 8:
	Scene 9:
	Scene 10:

Element of Setting

History, Culture, and Context:

Types of Settings:

Discovering Setting:

```
X W N I Q R G M A O C M P H W
T R A U D P C Z S Z Z E O M I
P O R D K C A B F I R R B O Z
I R R C T M N Q K F L C I F D
R M A A V E M E O Z L A A U O
C C T K Z T M R E A B R E R F
S T I D I S M P C R S P O R P
W H V M L A R I O O U O Z A P
V E E Z N R R Z C R Z T V G K
Q A B C C O O J H R A N L D X
D T E M T E E W X O K L Q U Y
K E F S G L A U S I V S N Y C
Q R I A K C L O K I Z U K V A
R H T H U O L O C A T I O N R
T S T Y L I Z A T I O N O D E
```

backdrop	narrative	stylization
culture	performance	temporal
era	props	theater
historical	realism	time
location	script	visual
mood	stage	world

Settings and Life-Circles

Impact of Setting on Characters:

Habits and Routines:

Setting As a Character:

Post Questions:

How might a rural setting differ from an urban one in shaping a character's daily life in musical theater?

Can you give an example of a musical where the setting acts almost like a character?

How do historical settings influence the routines and habits of characters in musical theater?

(doodle space)

Study: Settings

Choose three scenes or monologues. Describe the situation, then provide as many details on the setting as you can find, using the prompts to guide you.

Scene:	Description:	Setting:
		Time Period:
		Location:
		Mood and Atmosphere:
	Who are the important characters and how do they interact with the setting?	
Scene:	Description:	Setting:
		Time Period:
		Location:
		Mood and Atmosphere:
	Who are the important characters and how do they interact with the setting?	
Scene:	Description:	Setting:
		Time Period:
		Location:
		Mood and Atmosphere:
	Who are the important characters and how do they interact with the setting?	

Characters in Settings

What a Character Brings:

What a Setting Brings:

Interplay Between Settings and Characters:

Post Questions:

Describe how an aspect of setting might affect a character's behavior.

Imagine a change in the setting of a musical. Identify the musical and how you think the change in setting would impact the work.

How might a character's familiarity with a setting change their behavior in it? Give a specific example.

(doodle space)

Inner Theater vs Outer Theater

Exploring Inner Theater:

Navigating Outer Theater:

Choosing Targets of Focus:

Post Questions:

Think of a recent performance or rehearsal. How did your awareness of external sensory inputs (like lighting, sound, or audience reactions) affect your performance?

How can managing inner and outer theater help with the internalization process?

What is meant by a **resonant connection**?

(doodle space)

Developing Outer Theater

Meaning of Outer Theater:

Attention Targets:

Area and Intensity of Focus:

Post Questions:

How can an actor's focus on different attention targets affect their interaction with other characters on stage?

How can shifting focus enhance a performance?

How does the combination of attention targets and outer theater contribute to the overall effectiveness of a musical theater performance?

(doodle space)

Study: Drawing Dramatic Shape

Identify ten important moments throughout the play and use those to graph the dramatic shape of the entire show. Describe each moment's importance and intensity level, then graph them in order on the graph. Make sure to include all the most important plot or character changes.

1	2	3	4	5	6	7	8	9	10

1
2
3
4
5
6
7
8
9
10

Physical Theater

Inner Theater:

Outer Theater:

Physical Theater:

Method of Actions and Activities

Actions vs Activities:

Discovering Actions and Activities:

Physical Rehearsal and Kinesthetic Memory:

Post Questions:

Give an example of an action and contrast it with an activity.

Describe how improvisation can help a performer discover unique actions and activities for their character.

What is meant by the word **kinesthetic**?

(doodle space)

Convergent Inner and Outer Theater

Performance Theater:

Convergent Choices:

Convergent Rehearsal:

```
N J F V Z C Q R D B I O E O U E S K
X L N J C S O I E E R D M U N L C P
Y C L P L H R N S N E U U T J B R R
T H E A T E R Z V W N G T E U M I C
X Z Y J C U F Y M E F I S R M E P I
S S F T V Q P R R N R H O D X S T H
E E O V D A I E C T I G C L S N L X
C R Q V D L A S R A E H E R E E W E
C H A R A C T E R F R Y I N R B S M
P B R X E Z S V B C O W P X T I K O
M C O N B U M W W P T R J S V B S T
D V P N H G G H R Q T P M O G G H I
F U U S N U L O L A D H R A A L N O
Z R D I Q Q P F L U V P E M N D F N
H W T P K S Y N K O M J A A B C G N
R C I E G A T S X I N R W G T T E M
A B A C K D R O P T D O R H C E V Z
N M M Q Y Y W F C S Z X M L N K R W
```

acting	costume	monologue
character	drama	ensemble
convergent	theater	improvise
script	performance	backdrop
director	outer	theater
rehearsal	props	emotion
inner	stage	

Guided Study: Aligning Inner and Outer Theater

Scene and Character:		
Lines:	**Inner Target:**	**Outer Target:**

Study: Aligning Inner and Outer Theater

Dialogue:	Inner Theater:	Outer Theater:

Study: Final Sequence Plan

Number the lines or ideas of your script, and keep the numbered script with your plan. For each line or idea, identify either inner or outer theater, an action or activity, and a target and exchange of resources. **All lines must be accounted for, even if your character is not speaking.**

Lines:	Inner/Outer Theater	Action/Activity	Target/Communion

Lines:	Inner/Outer Theater	Action/Activity	Target/Communion

Performing a Routine

Exact Sequences:

High-Skill Sequences:

Mastering Skills and Sequences:

Vaudeville Viewing

Character: How does "character" seem related to vaudeville performances? How do the performers take advantage of this element?
Skilled Sequences: How difficult do you think the performance is? What parts, if any, required a significant amount of convergent practice?
Spectacle: How does "spectacle" seem related to vaudeville performances? How do the performers take advantage of this element?
Plot: How significant is story and narrative in vaudeville performance? How do performers use this element in their work?

Literary Analysis: Genre & Tradition

Analysis of Tradition:
Genres:
Post Questions:
How does written language affect the development of a tradition?
How is a literary tradition different from a custom?
Name a few genres of theater or film. Choose one and identify some aspects of it that you either enjoy or dislike.

Modern Age

Cultural/Social Analysis:

Modern Age:

Film, Video, and the Internet:

The Broadway Musical

Reverse History Approach:

120 Years of Broadway:

Active Viewing Notes:

Post Questions:

What are some advantages of the *backwards through traditions* approach to history?

What might be disadvantages of the approach?

Where is Broadway located, and why is it significant to modern theater?

(doodle space)

Broadway Since 2000

Multi-Million Dollar Budgets:

Broadway Since 2000:

Active Viewing Notes:

Post Questions:

What are some reasons theater on Broadway is so competitive?

What are potentially "safe" sources Broadway producers rely on to make their money back?

How does innovation stay alive in theater when competition is so expensive?

(doodle space)

Broadway in the 1990s

Disney Dollars:
Influence of *Rent*:

Active Viewing Notes:

Post Questions:

Name two of Disney's successful Broadway musicals in the 1990s.

What is the prestigious award that is considered theater's version of the Oscar?

What was one reason Disney was able to enter Broadway competitively despite the cost of large productions?

(doodle space)

Broadway in the 1980s

London's West End:

MegaMusicals:

Active Viewing Notes:

Post Questions:

What theatrical region is considered Broadway's biggest competitor and where is it located?

What are two characteristics of a **megamusical**?

What was the name of the soprano who originated the character of Christine in Andrew Lloyd Webber's *Phantom of the Opera* and eventually married the composer?

(doodle space)

Broadway in the 1970s

Record Label Influence:

End of "Golden Age":

Active Viewing Notes:

Post Questions:

How did popular music influence the content of musicals in the 1970s?

Compare and contrast a 1970s **album musical** with a modern **jukebox musical**.

Name a musical from the 1970s or later that references or reminisces about the Golden Age of musicals.

(doodle space)

Broadway's Golden Age

Between Two Wars:

1943: *Oklahoma!*

1964: *Fiddler on the Roof*

Active Viewing Notes:

Post Questions:

What are some typical qualities of escapist entertainment?

What combination of elements makes a play a **book musical**?

What makes a *dream ballet* or *dream sequence* such an effective part of a book musical?

1930s: Musicals in the Movies

<u>End of 1920s:</u>

<u>Movies with Sound and Color:</u>

Active Viewing Notes:

Post Questions:

What are two reasons Broadway struggled to succeed in the 1930s?

What innovation achieved by Walt Disney was necessary to create musicals in film?

In what way did *Show Boat* foreshadow Broadway's Golden Age, even though it was 25 years earlier?

(doodle space)

The Roaring Twenties

The Roaring Twenties:
Ziegfeld Follies:

Active Viewing Notes:

Post Questions:

What are some examples of how American lifestyles were undergoing major changes in the 1920s?

What were some typical features of a Ziegfeld Follies production?

How did vaudeville influence the type of musical theater performed in the 1920s?

(doodle space)

Broadway 1910-1920

Broadway 1910-1920:

Emergence of Modern Musical:

Active Viewing Notes:

Post Questions:

What were the three competing influences in Broadway theater at the beginning of the 1900s?

How was an operetta different from the musical comedies of the time?

Which of these three influences do you think had the most impact on today's Broadway theater? Why?

(doodle space)

Broadway in 1900 (and Today)

Beginnings of Broadway:

Times Square:

Timeline:

1900
1910
1920
1930
1940
1950
1960
1970
1980
1990
2000
2010

Section II:

Rehearsal and Improvisation Journal

DATE:

Participant: ☐ (role)________________________________ Audience: ☐

Scene or Scenario:	Active Focuses or Expectations:

Results and Post-Considerations:

DATE:

Participant: ☐ (role)________________________________ Audience: ☐

Scene or Scenario:	Active Focuses or Expectations:

Results and Post-Considerations:

DATE:

Participant: ☐ (role)________________________________ Audience: ☐

Scene or Scenario:	Active Focuses or Expectations:

Results and Post-Considerations:

DATE:

Participant: ☐ (role)________________________________ Audience: ☐

Scene or Scenario:	Active Focuses or Expectations:

Results and Post-Considerations:

DATE:

Participant: ☐ (role)________________________________ Audience: ☐

Scene or Scenario:	Active Focuses or Expectations:

Results and Post-Considerations:

DATE:

Participant: ☐ (role)________________________________ Audience: ☐

Scene or Scenario:	Active Focuses or Expectations:

Results and Post-Considerations:

DATE:

Participant: ☐ (role)____________________________ Audience: ☐

Scene or Scenario:	Active Focuses or Expectations:

Results and Post-Considerations:

DATE:

Participant: ☐ (role)____________________________ Audience: ☐

Scene or Scenario:	Active Focuses or Expectations:

Results and Post-Considerations:

<u>DATE:</u>

Participant: ☐ (role)________________________________ Audience: ☐

Scene or Scenario:	Active Focuses or Expectations:

Results and Post-Considerations:

<u>DATE:</u>

Participant: ☐ (role)________________________________ Audience: ☐

Scene or Scenario:	Active Focuses or Expectations:

Results and Post-Considerations:

<table>
<tr><td colspan="2">DATE:

Participant: ☐ (role)________________________________ Audience: ☐</td></tr>
<tr><td>Scene or Scenario:</td><td>Active Focuses or Expectations:</td></tr>
<tr><td colspan="2">Results and Post-Considerations:</td></tr>
</table>

<table>
<tr><td colspan="2">DATE:

Participant: ☐ (role)________________________________ Audience: ☐</td></tr>
<tr><td>Scene or Scenario:</td><td>Active Focuses or Expectations:</td></tr>
<tr><td colspan="2">Results and Post-Considerations:</td></tr>
</table>

<table>
<tr><td colspan="2">DATE:

Participant: ☐ (role)________________________________ Audience: ☐</td></tr>
<tr><td>Scene or Scenario:</td><td>Active Focuses or Expectations:</td></tr>
<tr><td colspan="2">Results and Post-Considerations:</td></tr>
<tr><td colspan="2">DATE:

Participant: ☐ (role)________________________________ Audience: ☐</td></tr>
<tr><td>Scene or Scenario:</td><td>Active Focuses or Expectations:</td></tr>
<tr><td colspan="2">Results and Post-Considerations:</td></tr>
</table>

DATE: Participant: ☐ (role)________________________ Audience: ☐	
Scene or Scenario:	Active Focuses or Expectations:
Results and Post-Considerations:	

DATE: Participant: ☐ (role)________________________ Audience: ☐	
Scene or Scenario:	Active Focuses or Expectations:
Results and Post-Considerations:	

DATE:

Participant: ☐ (role)________________________________ Audience: ☐

Scene or Scenario:	Active Focuses or Expectations:

Results and Post-Considerations:

DATE:

Participant: ☐ (role)________________________________ Audience: ☐

Scene or Scenario:	Active Focuses or Expectations:

Results and Post-Considerations:

DATE:

Participant: ☐ (role)______________________________ Audience: ☐

Scene or Scenario:	Active Focuses or Expectations:

Results and Post-Considerations:

DATE:

Participant: ☐ (role)______________________________ Audience: ☐

Scene or Scenario:	Active Focuses or Expectations:

Results and Post-Considerations:

DATE:

Participant: ☐ (role)________________________________ Audience: ☐

Scene or Scenario:	Active Focuses or Expectations:

Results and Post-Considerations:

DATE:

Participant: ☐ (role)________________________________ Audience: ☐

Scene or Scenario:	Active Focuses or Expectations:

Results and Post-Considerations:

DATE: Participant: ☐ (role)______________________________ Audience: ☐	
Scene or Scenario:	Active Focuses or Expectations:
Results and Post-Considerations:	

DATE: Participant: ☐ (role)______________________________ Audience: ☐	
Scene or Scenario:	Active Focuses or Expectations:
Results and Post-Considerations:	

<u>DATE:</u>

Participant: ☐ (role)________________________________	Audience: ☐
Scene or Scenario:	Active Focuses or Expectations:
Results and Post-Considerations:	

<u>DATE:</u>

Participant: ☐ (role)________________________________	Audience: ☐
Scene or Scenario:	Active Focuses or Expectations:
Results and Post-Considerations:	

DATE:

Participant: ☐ (role)________________________________ Audience: ☐

Scene or Scenario:	Active Focuses or Expectations:

Results and Post-Considerations:

DATE:

Participant: ☐ (role)________________________________ Audience: ☐

Scene or Scenario:	Active Focuses or Expectations:

Results and Post-Considerations:

DATE:

Participant: ☐ (role)______________________________ Audience: ☐

Scene or Scenario:	Active Focuses or Expectations:

Results and Post-Considerations:

DATE:

Participant: ☐ (role)______________________________ Audience: ☐

Scene or Scenario:	Active Focuses or Expectations:

Results and Post-Considerations:

DATE:

Participant: ☐ (role)____________________________________ Audience: ☐

Scene or Scenario:	Active Focuses or Expectations:

Results and Post-Considerations:

DATE:

Participant: ☐ (role)____________________________________ Audience: ☐

Scene or Scenario:	Active Focuses or Expectations:

Results and Post-Considerations:

DATE: Participant: ☐ (role)________________________________ Audience: ☐	
Scene or Scenario:	Active Focuses or Expectations:
Results and Post-Considerations:	

DATE: Participant: ☐ (role)________________________________ Audience: ☐	
Scene or Scenario:	Active Focuses or Expectations:
Results and Post-Considerations:	

DATE:

Participant: ☐ (role)________________________________ Audience: ☐

Scene or Scenario:	Active Focuses or Expectations:

Results and Post-Considerations:

DATE:

Participant: ☐ (role)________________________________ Audience: ☐

Scene or Scenario:	Active Focuses or Expectations:

Results and Post-Considerations:

DATE:

Participant: ☐ (role)______________________ Audience: ☐

Scene or Scenario:	Active Focuses or Expectations:

Results and Post-Considerations:

DATE:

Participant: ☐ (role)______________________ Audience: ☐

Scene or Scenario:	Active Focuses or Expectations:

Results and Post-Considerations:

DATE:

Participant: ☐ (role)______________________________ Audience: ☐

Scene or Scenario:	Active Focuses or Expectations:

Results and Post-Considerations:

DATE:

Participant: ☐ (role)______________________________ Audience: ☐

Scene or Scenario:	Active Focuses or Expectations:

Results and Post-Considerations:

DATE: Participant: ☐ (role)______________________________ Audience: ☐	
Scene or Scenario:	Active Focuses or Expectations:
Results and Post-Considerations:	

DATE: Participant: ☐ (role)______________________________ Audience: ☐	
Scene or Scenario:	Active Focuses or Expectations:
Results and Post-Considerations:	

DATE:	
Participant: ☐ (role)________________________	Audience: ☐
Scene or Scenario:	Active Focuses or Expectations:
Results and Post-Considerations:	

DATE:	
Participant: ☐ (role)________________________	Audience: ☐
Scene or Scenario:	Active Focuses or Expectations:
Results and Post-Considerations:	

DATE:

Participant: ☐ (role)____________________________ Audience: ☐

Scene or Scenario:	Active Focuses or Expectations:

Results and Post-Considerations:

DATE:

Participant: ☐ (role)____________________________ Audience: ☐

Scene or Scenario:	Active Focuses or Expectations:

Results and Post-Considerations:

DATE:

Participant: ☐ (role)______________________________ Audience: ☐

Scene or Scenario:	Active Focuses or Expectations:

Results and Post-Considerations:

DATE:

Participant: ☐ (role)______________________________ Audience: ☐

Scene or Scenario:	Active Focuses or Expectations:

Results and Post-Considerations:

Section III:

Active Focuses and Skill Games

Active Focuses

Off-Page Reading

A preliminary active focus technique in theater, used during the initial stages of script reading and rehearsal. This method involves actors holding the script in hand but requires them to lift their eyes from the page as they deliver their lines. The emphasis is on beginning the process of internalizing and understanding the dialogue in terms of coherent ideas and themes from the outset.

- Enhances early comprehension and memorization of the script.
- Promotes an immediate engagement with the narrative and character development.
- Encourages actors to start thinking about the dialogue in terms of larger ideas and emotional arcs.
- Ideal for actors in the preliminary stages of rehearsal, helping them transition smoothly from reading to performing.
- Useful in fostering a collaborative and responsive atmosphere among the cast from the beginning of the rehearsal process.

Initial Script Interaction: During early readings, actors are allowed to hold the script. However, they are encouraged to familiarize themselves with their lines to a degree where they can momentarily look away from the script as they speak. This technique bridges the gap between reading and performing, facilitating a gradual transition from script dependence to memorization.

Encouraging Idea Grouping: By lifting their eyes from the script while delivering lines, actors start to group the dialogue into coherent ideas and themes. This approach promotes an early understanding of the narrative and character motivations. It aids in identifying the natural flow and emotional beats of the dialogue, encouraging a deeper connection with the text.

Building Memory and Connection: Off-Page Reading is an effective way to begin internalizing the script. It challenges actors to recall lines and cues, strengthening memory and recall skills. This technique also fosters a stronger connection with fellow actors early in the rehearsal process, as it encourages more eye contact and responsive interaction.

Application in Early Rehearsals: Particularly useful in the initial stages of rehearsal, this method sets a foundation for a more engaged and interactive reading of the script. It is a crucial step before moving on to more advanced memorization techniques like the "Off-Book" method.

Off-Book

An essential active focus technique in theater that involves performing from memory, without the aid of a script. This approach is crucial in the early stages of rehearsal as it lays a solid foundation for character and scene development. Depending on the specific requirements of a rehearsal or director, the off-book stage may include allowances for calling lines or incorporating improvisation to enhance the flow of ideas.

- Accelerates mastery and fosters a comprehensive grasp of the script.
- Enhances presence and authenticity in the actor's performance.
- Encourages early and continuous exploration of character depth and scene dynamics.
- Essential for actors at all stages, especially beneficial in the initial phases of rehearsal to establish a strong, internalized understanding of the material.
- Helps in creating a more dynamic and fluid rehearsal process, laying the groundwork for subsequent developmental layers.

Early Memorization: Actors are encouraged to memorize their lines and cues as early as possible in the rehearsal process. This early internalization provides a consistent foundation upon which all other aspects of character and scene development are built. Emphasis on memorization from the beginning fosters a deeper and more immediate connection with the material.

Flexibility with Line Calling: Depending on the rehearsal approach, actors may be allowed to call for lines if needed. This practice can be a helpful tool in the learning process, aiding in the smooth recovery and continuation of the scene during memory lapses. In more rigorous settings, line calling might be limited to encourage stronger memorization.

Incorporating Improvisation: Early stages of being off-book may permit improvisation around the script's ideas. This approach allows actors to explore different interpretations and nuances of their character, enhancing the natural flow of the performance. Improvisation serves as a creative tool to deepen understanding and add layers to the character and scene.

Foundational Role in Performance Preparation: Adopting an off-book approach early in the rehearsal process is vital for establishing a solid base for character and scene work. It enables actors to focus more on interaction, expression, and the physicality of their performance, free from the distraction of a script.

Fast As Possible

Emphasizes speed in delivering lines and executing cues. This method is geared towards rehearsing a scene or monologue at an accelerated pace, with the goal of minimizing conscious reflection and overcoming memory barriers to enhance fluidity in performance.

- Helps actors to overcome mental blocks and memory issues by encouraging rapid recall.
- Enhances the overall fluidity and pace of the performance.
- Useful in developing an actor's ability to stay focused and responsive under pressure.
- Suitable for actors of all levels who are looking to improve their memorization skills and the pacing of their performances.

Rapid Delivery: Actors are instructed to perform their lines and execute their cues as quickly as they can, pushing beyond their usual pace. The focus is on speed and immediacy, rather than on perfect articulation or emotional expression.

Minimizing Reflection: By moving rapidly through the material, actors allow little time for conscious thought or reflection. This approach aims to reduce overthinking and promotes a more instinctual performance. The technique helps in identifying areas where the actor may be hesitating or struggling with recall.

Promoting Memorization and Flow: The fast-paced nature of this exercise aids in solidifying memorization, as actors are forced to recall lines and cues quickly. It also helps in identifying the natural flow of the scene or monologue, as pauses and hesitations are minimized.

Application in Rehearsal: This technique can be used during rehearsals for both monologues and scenes. It is particularly useful for breaking down mental barriers and promoting a smoother transition between lines and actions.

Amplified Self

Emphasizes a deepened sensory engagement during a performance. This approach involves an acute awareness and magnification of the actor's sensory experiences on stage, allowing for a more immersive and authentic portrayal.

- Deepens the actor's connection to their character and the stage environment.
- Facilitates a more nuanced and authentic portrayal, as reactions are rooted in real sensory experiences.
- Encourages spontaneity and naturalism in performances.
- Ideal for actors looking to enrich their performances with a more genuine and spontaneous expression.
- Particularly useful in immersive theater settings or pieces that demand a strong sense of presence and realism.

Personal Connection: The actor begins by introspectively connecting with their own emotions and experiences, relating them to the character's situation. This connection serves as the foundation for the performance, grounding the actor in reality while preparing them for emotional amplification.

Amplification of Reactions: Once this personal connection is established, the actor amplifies their natural reactions. These reactions, while rooted in genuine emotion, are exaggerated to suit the theatrical context. The exaggeration is not merely for effect but is a deliberate and controlled enhancement to convey the intensity of emotions more powerfully to the audience.

Application in Monologues and Scenes: This technique can be applied in both monologues and multi-character scenes. In monologues, it allows for a more dynamic and engaging solo performance, as the actor's amplified emotions add depth and nuance. In scenes, it enriches interactions between characters, as each actor's amplified self contributes to a more vibrant and emotionally charged exchange.

Inhabiting States of Being

Revolves around maintaining a consistent emotional or psychological state throughout an improvisation or rehearsal. This method requires actors to deeply immerse themselves in a particular state-of-being, or a predetermined sequence of states, ensuring that their performance consistently reflects these emotional conditions.

- Fosters a deeper, more consistent character portrayal.
- Enhances the actor's emotional awareness and control.
- Aids in creating a more believable and relatable character by ensuring emotional authenticity and depth.
- Suitable for actors looking to deepen their emotional engagement with their characters and improve their ability to sustain complex emotional states.
- Beneficial in rehearsals and performances that require a strong focus on character psychology and emotional continuity.

Establishing the State of Being: The process begins with the actor identifying and understanding the specific state-of-being their character is in. This could range from a single dominant emotion or mood to a more complex psychological condition. In cases of a sequence of states, the actor prepares to transition smoothly between different emotional or psychological conditions as dictated by the script or scene.

Consistent Emotional Immersion: During performance or rehearsal, the actor focuses on sustaining this chosen state-of-being, allowing it to inform every aspect of their portrayal - from dialogue delivery to physical expression. The challenge lies in maintaining this emotional consistency, regardless of the external stimuli or interactions occurring in the scene.

Adaptation Within the State: While staying true to the core state-of-being, the actor must also adapt and respond to the unfolding scene or improvisation. This requires a balance between maintaining the internal state and reacting naturally to external factors. In sequences, the actor navigates the emotional arc with fluidity, ensuring each transition is motivated and seamless.

Application in Practice: This technique is particularly useful in scenes where emotional continuity is key, or in character studies focusing on the exploration of specific psychological conditions. It enhances the actor's ability to stay deeply connected with their character's internal world, even amidst a dynamic and changing external environment.

Amplified Experience

Centers on enhancing and magnifying an actor's personal reactions and emotions during a performance. This approach bridges the gap between the actor's authentic self and the character they portray, creating a deeply resonant and exaggerated expression of emotions.

- Helps explore and build personal resources as a performer.
- Facilitates a more authentic and relatable portrayal of characters.

- Enhances emotional depth and engagement in a performance.
- Encourages actors to explore and express a wider range of emotions, leading to more dynamic and compelling performances.
- Suitable for actors seeking to deepen their emotional connection to their roles and enhance their expressive capabilities.
- Particularly beneficial in dramatic pieces where emotional intensity and depth are crucial.

Enhanced Sensory Awareness: Actors are encouraged to intensify their awareness of the five senses—sight, sound, touch, smell, and taste—within the context of their performance. This heightened sensory attention involves closely observing the stage environment, listening to the nuances of sound, and being acutely aware of physical sensations.

Engagement with On-Stage Elements: Performers are prompted to fully immerse themselves in their immediate surroundings, letting themselves be drawn into, and even momentarily distracted by, on-stage stimuli. This engagement allows for a more organic and spontaneous reaction to the environment, adding realism to the performance.

Selective Focus: While deeply involved with on-stage experiences, actors maintain a disciplined focus, keeping off-stage elements outside their sphere of attention. This selective focus ensures that the performance remains grounded and centered, preventing overstimulation or loss of character.

Targeted Self

Encourages actors to concentrate on specific parts of their body as a means to channel distinct types of expression during a performance. This method allows actors to connect more deeply with various aspects of their character's psyche and emotion.

- Encourages a holistic approach to character portrayal, integrating physical, emotional, intellectual, and social elements.
- Enhances the depth and complexity of the performance, providing a more layered and textured expression.
- Aids actors in accessing and portraying a wide range of emotions and thoughts, leading to a more dynamic and engaging performance.
- Suitable for actors seeking to explore and embody the multi-dimensional aspects of their characters.
- Particularly beneficial for performances that require deep introspection and varied emotional expressions.

Body Part Focus: Actors select a specific part of their body (head, heart, stomach, or feet) as a focal point, each representing a different realm of expression.

- Head: Focuses on philosophical or intellectual aspects, stimulating thought-provoking and analytical expressions.
- Heart: Channels emotional or personal elements, enhancing the portrayal of feelings and inner turmoil.
- Stomach: Connects to physical and visceral responses, invoking instinctual and gut-driven reactions.
- Feet: Represents sociological or interpersonal dynamics, grounding the performance in social context and relations.

Communion with the Target Area: The actor seeks a deep communion with the chosen body part, either by drawing energy from it or directing energy towards it. This process involves a conscious effort to align the emotional and psychological state of the character with the physical locus.

Application in Monologues and Soliloquies: This technique is particularly effective in monologues or soliloquies, where the actor has the scope to delve into introspective and character-driven narratives. It allows for a nuanced exploration of the character's inner world, as the actor shifts focus between different body parts to express varying facets of the character's psyche.

Dynamics

Centers on the modulation and manipulation of an actor's intensity and energy levels during a performance. This technique is designed to create a more vibrant and impactful portrayal by actively adjusting the emotional and physical dynamics.

- Enhances the emotional depth and range of a performance.
- Encourages actors to remain present and responsive, adapting their performance to the evolving dynamics of the scene.
- Facilitates a more captivating and unpredictable portrayal, making the character's journey more compelling.
- Ideal for actors who wish to explore and expand their range of expressiveness and emotional depth.
- Particularly effective in dynamic and emotionally varied scripts where fluctuating intensities are crucial to the narrative.

Intensity Modulation: Actors are encouraged to consciously adjust the intensity of their emotional, mental, and physical states throughout the performance. This modulation involves fluctuating between different levels of energy, tension, and expressiveness, tailoring these elements to suit the narrative and dramatic context.

Spontaneous Dynamic Choices: The technique emphasizes making impromptu decisions regarding gestures, movements, and expressions, ensuring that each choice adds to the overall dynamism of the performance. These choices are made in the moment, guided by the actor's intuition and connection to the character and scene.

Creating Dynamic Gestures: Actors focus on crafting gestures that are not only expressive but also dynamically varied, ranging from subtle to pronounced, based on the needs of the scene. This approach allows for a physical manifestation of the internal dynamics, making the performance more engaging and visually compelling.

Application in Performances: Suitable for both monologues and interactive scenes, using dynamics adds an element of energy and vitality to the performance. It helps in creating a performance that is not monotonous but rather fluctuates in intensity, keeping the audience engaged and emotionally connected.

Through-Line Focus

Emphasizes the continuous and consistent pursuit of a character's primary objective throughout a scene or monologue. This active focus technique encourages actors to align every line, action, and reaction with their character's overarching goal, ensuring a coherent and purpose-driven performance.

- Promotes a deeper understanding and embodiment of the character's motivations and desires.
- Enhances the narrative clarity and emotional impact of the performance.
- Aids in creating a more engaging and believable portrayal, drawing the audience more deeply into the story.
- Ideal for actors seeking to develop a more nuanced and intentional approach to character portrayal.
- Particularly beneficial in performances where character objectives are complex or integral to the plot.

Identification of Objective: Actors begin by identifying their character's main objective or goal within the context of the scene or monologue. This objective is the driving force behind the character's actions and decisions. Understanding the character's objective provides clarity and direction to the performance.

Alignment with Objective: Every line delivered, gesture made, and emotion expressed is consciously tied to achieving the character's objective. This alignment ensures that each element of the performance contributes cohesively to the portrayal of the character's journey and desires.

Consistency and Coherence: Maintaining a through-line focus requires consistent attention to the character's objective throughout the performance, avoiding deviations that may detract from the primary goal. This consistency enhances the coherence and believability of the character, making their actions and motivations more understandable and relatable to the audience.

Application in Performances: This technique is applicable in both dramatic monologues and interactive scenes. In monologues, it aids in creating a focused and compelling solo performance. In scenes, it enriches the interaction between characters, as each actor's through-line focus contributes to a dynamic and purposeful exchange.

Environmental Awareness

Centers on the actor's engagement with their setting. This approach encourages actors to visualize, interact with, and enliven the environment around them, enhancing the realism and immersion of the performance for both themselves and the audience.

- Enhances the overall realism and depth of the performance.
- Helps in creating a more immersive and engaging experience for the audience.
- Aids actors in grounding their performance, providing a richer context for their character's actions and reactions.
- Suitable for actors of all levels, as it fosters a greater connection to the performance space and enhances the portrayal of the character within their environment.
- Particularly beneficial in productions where the setting plays a significant role in the narrative or character development.

Visualization of Setting: Actors begin by deeply visualizing the scene's setting, whether it's a detailed physical set or an imagined space. This visualization involves considering all aspects of the environment: spatial dimensions, objects present, sounds, smells, and the overall atmosphere.

Active Interaction with Environment: Actors are encouraged to physically and mentally interact with their surroundings. This can involve touching objects, reacting to imaginary stimuli, or moving through the space in ways that reflect the character's interaction with their environment. Such interactions help to ground the actor in the scene, making the performance more authentic and believable.

Bringing the Environment to Life: The goal is to make the environment come alive, not just for the actor but also for the audience. By engaging with the setting in a dynamic and realistic manner, actors help the audience visualize and believe in the world of the play.

Application in Performances: This technique is crucial in both rehearsal and performance settings. During practice, it aids in developing a strong sense of place and context for the character's actions. In performance, it enhances the believability of the scene and strengthens the audience's immersion in the story.

Discovery Theater

Emphasizes a profound engagement with both internal experiences and external stimuli. This method involves actors drawing connections between their personal memories or sensations and their character's experiences, while also being acutely aware of their surrounding theatrical environment.

- Promotes a deeper, more nuanced connection between the actor and their character.
- Enhances the actor's ability to draw upon personal experiences, adding authenticity to the performance.
- Encourages a comprehensive awareness of the performance space, enriching the actor's interaction with their environment.
- Suitable for actors at all levels, especially those seeking to develop a more introspective and responsive approach to their craft.
- Beneficial in both individual and ensemble work, as it fosters a deeper understanding of character and context.

Internal Engagement: During practice or performance, actors are encouraged to deeply engage with their own emotions, memories, and life experiences. They seek to identify and connect these personal elements with those of their character, finding parallels that help to deepen their understanding and portrayal.

Cataloging Resonant Experiences: Actors are advised to mentally catalogue experiences and sensations that particularly resonate with their character. This could include specific emotions, memories, or physical sensations. These resonant experiences are noted for later reflection and incorporation into rehearsal, enhancing the depth and authenticity of the character portrayal.

Sensory Awareness of the Outer Theater: Concurrently, actors maintain a heightened awareness of their external environment – the 'outer theater'. This includes noticing the set, props, lighting, sounds, and even the audience's reactions. Sensory points of interest that seem relevant or impactful to the character are mentally cataloged.

Journaling for Reflection: Post-performance or rehearsal, actors are encouraged to record these internal and external observations in a journal. This practice aids in consolidating the discoveries and reflections, making them more accessible for future rehearsals and performances.

Improvisation Games

Inner Monologue

This game can be played either solo or with multiple participants. It is particularly effective in exploring character depth and enhancing improvisational skills.

Objective: To express unfiltered thoughts and emotions of a character, bringing inner conflicts and perspectives to the forefront. It serves as a tool for actors to delve deeper into both themselves and their characters by vocalizing their inner thoughts.

Gameplay Variations:

Solo Performance (True Monologue): The actor performs alone, articulating every thought as it occurs. This variation focuses on the individual's ability to maintain a continuous stream of consciousness, offering a deeper understanding of the character's psyche.

Group Interaction (Multiple Players): Involves two or more actors, where they occasionally 'break the third wall' to articulate their character's inner thoughts amidst regular dialogue. This version allows for the juxtaposition of spoken dialogue and internal monologue, creating a complex layering of character interactions and motivations.

Cacophony (High Chaos Version): Involves three or more actors simultaneously speaking, mixing inner monologues with dialogues. The challenge is to maintain non-stop verbal expression while working towards a common scenario objective. This high-energy variant tests the actors' ability to multitask, stay in character, and react spontaneously to overlapping dialogues and monologues.

Live Broadcast

Simulates the dynamics of a live broadcast event. This game is engaging and often humorous, perfect for developing quick thinking and verbal dexterity.

Objective: To create a spontaneous and entertaining live broadcast scenario, with participants taking on the roles of announcers. The game emphasizes creativity, wit, and the ability to improvise commentary on the fly.

Instructions:

The game involves at least two players, each assuming the role of a broadcaster: one as the play-by-play announcer and the other as the color commentator. The scenario can be set as a radio broadcast, television show, or live event commentary.

Play-by-Play Announcer: This participant describes the unfolding events in real-time, focusing on the action and providing a detailed narrative of what is occurring. The role requires a focus on clarity, detail, and the ability to vividly paint a picture for the audience.

Color Commentator: This role involves adding personality, background information, humorous asides, and personal insights to the broadcast. The commentator complements the play-by-play by providing depth, humor, and a human touch to the narrative.

Event Selection: The event being broadcast can range from ordinary activities (like a cooking demonstration) to the absurd (such as an alien invasion). The choice of event significantly influences the tone and style of the commentary, allowing for a wide range of creative expression.

Applications:

Excellent for developing improvisational skills, particularly in the realms of quick thinking, verbal creativity, and collaborative storytelling. Useful in teaching the dynamics of broadcast media, including the distinct roles and styles of different types of announcers.

HyperColors

Utilizes colors as a means to represent and manipulate the intensity and dynamics of a performance. This game involves the use of colored lights, cards, or slides, offering a visually stimulating and engaging method to guide actors' emotional and energy levels.

Instructions:

Color Representation: Assign specific emotional or dynamic states to different colors. For instance, red could signify high energy or anger, blue could indicate calmness or sadness, yellow might represent happiness or excitement, etc. This color-coding helps actors quickly associate each color with a particular state-of-being.

Color Change Mechanism: Colors can be changed using lights, cards, or slides. The change can be controlled by a designated "director" or set on an automated timer. The frequency and sequence of color changes should be determined before the game begins.

Pre-Planned vs. Spontaneous Sequences: The color sequences can be pre-planned, allowing for the creation of a choreographed series of emotional and dynamic shifts. Alternatively, the director can change colors spontaneously, challenging actors to adapt instantly to new emotional states.

Actor Response: Upon each color change, actors must modulate their performance to align with the new color's assigned state-of-being. This modulation involves adjusting not only emotional expression but also physicality, vocal tone, and overall energy levels.

Creating Dramatic Shapes: By varying the color sequences, directors can create diverse "dramatic shapes" or patterns in the performance, ranging from gradual emotional crescendos to abrupt mood shifts. This aspect of the game emphasizes the fluidity and adaptability in theatrical performances.

Applications:

Ideal for training actors in emotional versatility and responsiveness. Enhances the ability to quickly shift between different emotional and dynamic states. Encourages a deeper understanding of how color and emotion can be intertwined in a performance.

Changing Circumstances

Designed to challenge actors' improvisational skills and their ability to adapt to evolving scenarios. This game involves periodic alterations or additions to the initial circumstances of a scene, requiring actors to continuously adjust their performances accordingly.

Instructions:

Initial Circumstance Setup: At the start, a set of circumstances is established for the scene or improvisation. These could include character backstories, emotional states, environmental factors, or specific events. Actors begin the scene by fully engaging with these initial circumstances, developing and exploring them through their performance.

Intervals for Change: The scene progresses for a predetermined amount of time before being interrupted. At regular intervals (decided beforehand), the facilitator or a designated 'director' introduces changes or additions to the existing circumstances.

Implementing New Circumstances: These new circumstances can be modifications of the existing ones or entirely new elements added to the scene. They may drastically or subtly alter the direction, tone, or emotional content of the scene.

Adaptation and Continuation: Upon each change, actors must quickly adapt their performances to reflect the new circumstances while maintaining the continuity of the scene. The challenge lies in seamlessly integrating the changes and continuing the narrative from where it left off.

Developing the Scenario: As the game progresses, actors are encouraged to deepen their engagement with the evolving circumstances, finding creative ways to incorporate the changes into the scene. This process tests the actors' ability to stay in character, think on their feet, and maintain narrative coherence amidst shifting dynamics.

Applications:

Excellent for honing improvisational skills and adaptability in performance. Helps actors learn to quickly process and react to new information while staying true to their character and the story. Encourages creative problem-solving and narrative development skills.

Improvisation in Multiple Movements

Revolves around a series of predefined dramatic or circumstantial changes, each initiating a new segment or "movement" in the improvisation. This game enhances actors' ability to adapt to shifting narrative elements and maintain coherence across diverse scenarios.

Instructions:

Preparation of Movements: Before the improvisation begins, a list of distinct dramatic or circumstantial changes is prepared. These changes serve as triggers for new movements within the improvisation. Each movement represents a shift in the narrative, emotional tone, character dynamics, or situational context.

Initiation of Movements: Movements can be transitioned in various ways:

- Timed Changes: Movements change at predetermined intervals, adding a rhythmic structure to the improvisation.
- Director-Led Changes: A facilitator or director signals the transition to a new movement, possibly in response to the unfolding scene.
- Objective-Based Changes: Movements shift upon the achievement of specific objectives set within the scene.

Performance Adaptation: Actors must swiftly adapt their performances to align with the new circumstances introduced at the beginning of each movement. The challenge is to seamlessly incorporate the changes while maintaining the integrity and continuity of the overall improvisation.

Developing the Narrative: As the improvisation progresses through different movements, actors are encouraged to explore and expand the narrative, adjusting their character portrayals and interactions to reflect the evolving scenario. This process tests the actors' versatility and creativity in building a cohesive and engaging story through changing contexts.

Applications:

Excellent for developing an actor's ability to think quickly and adapt to new scenarios. Fosters a deeper understanding of narrative flow and character development across varying situations. Enhances collaborative storytelling and group dynamics in performance.

Hello, Is Anyone Home?

Designed to enhance an actor's ability to visualize and interact with a non-existent, yet detailed environment. This game focuses on exploring an imaginary space as if it were real, fostering creativity and enhancing spatial awareness.

Instructions:

Role Assignment: Three players are assigned specific roles:

1. English Speaker: This player speaks only in English, initiating and responding to the conversation.
2. Fictional Language Speaker: This player communicates in a completely made-up language, using gibberish or nonsensical sounds that have no real-world meaning.

3. Translator: This player acts as the intermediary, pretending to translate between the English speaker and the fictional language speaker.

Translation Dynamics: The translator listens to both parties and creatively 'translates' the dialogue, often adding humorous or unexpected twists to the conversation. The translator's role is crucial in maintaining the flow of conversation, ensuring both humor and coherence.

Improvisation and Creativity: All players are encouraged to improvise and be as creative as possible. The fictional language speaker should use expressive gestures and intonations to convey their 'message'. The English speaker and the translator react and adapt to these improvisations, leading to potentially humorous and unexpected exchanges.

Applications:

Ideal for developing quick thinking and improvisational skills. Encourages creativity, effective communication, and the ability to adapt to unpredictable elements in performance. Provides a fun and engaging way to explore non-verbal communication cues and the nuances of translation.

I Need a Translator

Improvisation game that involves three players, each taking on distinct roles in a simulated multilingual conversation. This game is designed to challenge players' improvisational skills and creativity, while also fostering effective communication and teamwork.

Instructions:

Setting the Scene: The game begins with setting up an imaginary environment. This could be any space – a house, a castle, a spaceship, etc. The more detailed the description of the setting, the better. The actor is informed that they are about to explore an unoccupied space, delving into an environment that is rich with unseen details and histories.

Exploration and Interaction: The actor then begins to 'explore' this space, moving around the stage as if walking through the actual environment. They should interact with imaginary objects, open unseen doors, peer through invisible windows, react to sounds only they can hear, etc., making the unseen seem real.

Creating a Narrative: As the exploration continues, the actor is encouraged to create a narrative or backstory about the environment. This could involve discovering items, encountering unexpected features, or reacting to the ambiance of the space. The narrative helps in adding depth to the exploration, making it more engaging and believable.

Physical and Vocal Expression: The actor uses physical gestures and vocal expressions to convey their discoveries and reactions. The use of mime techniques can be particularly effective. This aspect challenges the actor to convey their experience vividly to the audience, using only their body language and voice.

Applications:

Ideal for developing an actor's ability to visualize and convincingly portray imaginary scenarios. Enhances spatial awareness, creative thinking, and the ability to convey a story without relying on physical props or sets.

Section IV:

Worksheets

Cycle of Mastery

Embarking on the path of learning in any field is akin to setting off on a grand adventure. It is a voyage that takes us through varied landscapes of understanding and ability. In musical theater, this journey involves not only the acquisition of specific technical skills but also the development of a deep-seated connection with the art form. To navigate this path effectively, it is crucial to recognize the "Phases of Experience," which serve as the milestones of our educational and personal growth.

These phases mark our transition from novices to adept practitioners and, eventually, to masters of our craft. They are not merely stages of learning but are experiences that shape our approach, our thinking, and our performance. Understanding these phases helps us to better comprehend our reactions to new information, our struggles with difficult techniques, and our triumphs when everything comes together harmoniously.

The Phases of Experience

Phase 1: Initial Immersion

At the outset, your introduction to musical theater might feel overwhelming. This stage is characterized by a sense of discomfort and unfamiliarity as you're exposed to the breadth of this art form. From understanding the nuances of character development to the technicalities of vocal projection and choreography, it's natural to feel lost amidst the new terminologies and concepts.

Phase 2: Acclimation

As you continue to engage with the material and participate in exercises, you will start to find your footing. The once perplexing aspects of musical theater begin to make sense, and a rudimentary understanding of its components takes root. Curiosity replaces confusion, leading to a proactive quest for knowledge. Questions will arise, signaling a burgeoning interest and a desire to delve deeper into the world of theater.

Phase 3: Routine Flow

With consistent practice and exploration, what was once erratic and unpredictable becomes familiar. You can anticipate the sequence of a rehearsal, understand the flow of a scene, and execute routines with increasing confidence. This stage is marked by a smoother integration of skills, although they may not yet be fully automatic. The classroom and the stage start to feel like second homes, venues where creativity is nurtured and honed.

Phase 4: Full Internalization

At this advanced stage of learning, the skills and techniques of musical theater are embedded within you. They manifest effortlessly, often mistaken as innate talent by onlookers. Your ability to perform complex routines and embody characters with depth and authenticity is a testament to the internalization of your craft. This proficiency is available at a moment's notice—so much so that you could "do this in my sleep."

Multi-Iterative Circular Routines

The concept of a "multi-iterative cycle" is central to understanding how deep, meaningful learning and skill development occur, particularly in complex fields such as musical theater. This concept moves away from the traditional linear model of learning, which suggests a straightforward progression from not knowing to proficiency. Instead, it embraces a more nuanced approach, recognizing that true mastery unfolds in a series of layers, each one revisiting and expanding upon the last.

Imagine if learning were like a spiral staircase. As you ascend, you circle around and revisit the same points, but each time you do, you're a little higher up, seeing things from a new perspective. This is the essence of the multi-iterative cycle—a dynamic, non-linear process that encourages repeated engagement with material from fresh angles, leading to a richer and more sophisticated understanding. In the context of musical theater, this multi-iterative cycle is particularly relevant. The process of mastering a role, a song, or a dance isn't about doing it once and moving on. It's about revisiting these elements repeatedly, each time with deeper insight and more nuanced technique. Through this cycle, a performer can explore various facets of their craft, refine their skills, and uncover layers of complexity in their performance.

This cyclical approach aligns with the natural rhythm of learning, where repetition with variation leads to the discovery of new connections and possibilities. It's not about mere repetition for its own sake; it's about engaging with the material on a deeper level with each iteration. Each cycle through the material is an opportunity to integrate feedback, reflect on experiences, and apply lessons learned, thereby enhancing one's performance and artistry. As we delve into the multi-iterative cycle, we'll explore how this approach fosters a rich, ongoing dialogue between the learner and their craft. It's a conversation that evolves over time, informed by experience, and driven by a commitment to continual growth and excellence. Whether you're a budding actor, a seasoned singer, or a dancer just starting out, the multi-iterative cycle is a powerful framework for achieving the pinnacle of your artistic potential.

Post Questions:

How does the initial immersion phase in musical theater help establish the foundation for more advanced skill development?

Can you identify a moment in your learning when you transitioned from acclimation to routine flow, and what triggered that shift?

In what ways do repeated engagements with material in the multi-iterative cycle contribute to the depth of a performer's understanding of their craft?

How does full internalization of a musical theater skill differ from simply being familiar with it, and what benefits does this deeper integration provide to a performer?

How does the multi-iterative cycle differ from a more traditional, linear approach to learning?

Internalization

What Does It Mean to Have Something Internalized?

To have something internalized means it has become a natural or automatic part of you. It no longer requires thought or effort; it happens automatically when needed or desired. When achieved, you might say what you have internalized has become a part of your **active self** or personality.

Usually, it takes a very long time to internalize something. To achieve internalization requires effort, interest, and repetition, but once it is internalized these are no longer required. When something is internalized it is easy and natural, and seems more like a talent than something that has been learned. Both mental and physical things can be internalized, though the process is not exactly the same.

How Much Should I Practice?

The goal of practice is always to internalize something physical. Practice requires moving around, as it is impossible to internalize something physical without moving, but that does not mean it is the same as exercising. Also, practice does not really mean repeating things over and over and over again exactly the same (although repeating it is usually required). Instead practice means that you are trying to make physical motions more and more automatic, so that you don't have to think about them at all.

So, it is less about how *much* you should practice, and more about whether it is becoming or has become automatic.

Do I Need to Study?

The goal of study is also always to internalize, but instead of physical things, we study to internalize mental things. Studying requires thinking, as it is impossible to internalize something mental without thinking about it, but that does not mean it is the same as memorizing. Studying does not require moving around, though moving around might be helpful to study some things. But study is certainly not exercising muscles.

We want mental things often to be as automatic as physical things. Yes, studying is required, until certain concepts, thoughts, or inner models are internalized and appear in the mind automatically.

Goal-Oriented Study and Practice:

Remember, the goal is always to internalize. Learning is only temporary until you have reviewed material enough that you are able to access it automatically. Whether you are studying a concept, memorizing information, or improving a physical routine, mastery only comes when it has become a part of your active self.

Once something has been mastered, you can think more critically, consider more deeply, see solutions more intuitively, and operate with ease. Internalization allows you to rely on the foundation you have learned, so that you can achieve the real goal in performance: truly engaging with the material as though you have become one with it.

Post Questions:

What is the difference between study and practice?

How do you know if something has been internalized?

Is it more necessary to practice (and internalize physical things) or to study (and internalize mental things)? Justify your answer.

What is the single goal of both study and practice?

(doodle space)

The Script

Dialogue and Stage Directions:

When given a script, an actor has two initial responsibilities. The first is to make sure that they understand and can pronounce all the **dialogue** (the words spoken by the characters), and the second is to make sure they can visualize all the **stage directions** (the actions described in the text) and know what is supposed to happen on stage.

Words and Actions:

Dialogue refers to anything that is spoken (or sung – also called lyrics) in a stage production. When you first get a script, you should go through the dialogue and look for unfamiliar words. Even if you've seen it before and think you know what it means, if you have any doubts about how it is being used or how it should be pronounced you should still look it up. Start by going through the script and circling anything unfamiliar or hard to make sense of. Then, a website such as **www.dictionary.com** can supply you with both the definition and the pronunciation.

If it is an unfamiliar name, place, technical term, *et cetera*, then you might need to go farther than **dictionary.com**. A website like **www.wikipedia.com** or other similar resource, while not citable in a research paper, can be appropriate for your job as an actor, as it could provide cultural context or give you a place to start looking for dramatic ideas. Such resources can also jump-start deeper research, especially into modern or current theater trends, by providing names, dates, or other information that can be followed up in academic or peer-reviewed journals.

After familiarizing yourself with a new word or concept, practice pronouncing or rehearsing it until you can say it with confidence, so you don't hesitate or stumble in a **read-through.**

As an actor, it is not enough to just deliver the words of the dialogue. Remember, when you deliver the lines in the final production, they must seem like they came out of your own head and were spontaneously generated in response to what's happening on stage. If you cannot present the words with ease, it will be difficult to convince an audience the line came from your own mind.

Also, always keep in mind that is the responsibility of the actor for legal licensing purposes to follow the script exactly as written. No changes are allowed to dialogue without the written permission of the author or licensing agent. Only they can legally make such changes – not the producer, not the director, or any actor. In professional theater, improvisation is not allowed unless the script provides for it. While this rule is not always followed at an educational or community theater level, it is a strict rule in all professional theater productions or theaters can be forced to stop operating.

Stage directions – the parts of the script that describe the on-stage action – should also be followed as closely as possible, but adjustments may sometimes need to be made by necessity. In such cases, as long as the intent or original meaning remains unchanged, practical considerations are allowed for.

You don't have to worry about stage directions during a first read-through, but early on, you should still attempt to visualize the scene in your head as much as you are able. Authors may make references in stage directions to specific theatrical elements or other works to help explain their vision. Again, if these are unfamiliar to you or you are unsure of the context, make sure to look them up.

Post Questions:

Where might you go to learn how to pronounce an unfamiliar word?

How can a non-academic site like Wikipedia still be useful for an actor?

What are the first steps an actor should take when presented with a new script?

Who all is allowed to make changes to dialogue?

If stage directions need to be changed by necessity, what should stay the same?

K W H G H I G L J A P H T M L Y Q Z G O
Y S C O S T P J T O G P N L O E Z E I F
L V N W P Q U K C U I Z L K A A B Q R T
N G X Z X B S W O R K G I T D N J B V F
O L B C Q Z U R C W Q W J D D F T X B X
I Y Z C G Q H S I I L Y X W T H X U W D
T R M O N T R V U I B I A W B I I D H I
A I S P D R O X S E T Z Z B A W S G C A
I C D A W G T W D N A I D E P I K I W L
C O E E L E C Q V H O P I X N R K D V O
N R Q E A O A I K V Q I B B B J K L B G
U O D I R S S Q Y D I C T I O N A R Y U
N Q A Y G U A C L H O N Z C C L F T G E
O C N S A X I W Q T C Z M O E I C I D C
R I O L N S E Z Y Z K Q Y D X R T Q S P
P O I N T O T I Z W Y A T U G S I Q O L
C Z P V T T I R N C O M A C T J Y D X O
E M G M S E S T W O R D S A J X V W H K
K R V A I A X A C K B S G K A E N W K R
W I Z I R R R T R A L E L A O G A G T T

directions	dialogue	script
pronunciation	visualize	words
read-through	wikipedia	ideas
dictionary	actions	lyric
context	actor	stage

(doodle space)

Circumstances

Konstantin Stanislavski developed his acting method during his time as an actor and director in Russia. He had a passion for understanding the psychology of human beings and used this knowledge to develop an acting method that would help actors create real, believable characters. Stanislavski believed that actors should unite the expectations of a script with their own experiences and imagination when creating characters. His approach to acting is often referred to as "**method acting**," as he tried to present a systematic method for using experience and imagination to bring authenticity to stage performance.

An important aspect of Stanislavski's system is its reliance on **analysis**. Stanislavski believed that actors should analyze every aspect of a script and character, including their relationships, motivations, conflicts and goals.

An essential part of this analysis is the uncovering of **circumstances**, meaning all the conditions in which the action takes place. A character's motivation depends on their circumstances - those facts of life that created them, that shaped their development, and that continue to influence their decision making. It's important to understand, though, that when we talk about circumstances, we're generally stating facts about the surrounding or physical world, and not inner states like thoughts and emotions.

States of mind and being are also important parts of Stanislavski's analysis, but developing these come after first identifying the surrounding circumstances that created the situation to begin with.

Given Circumstances:

"Given circumstances" refer to the circumstances that are essential to the play or scene and must be followed, and therefore are written directly into the play or stated directly by the author. For example, a cast of characters may specify that "Gary is a balding, slightly overweight man in his forties." This is the most direct type of given circumstance, and these types of brief descriptions are common. But other things may also be given elsewhere in the script.

If the stage directions directly state anything about a character, it should be added to the list of given circumstances for that scene or moment. A particular element of costume may be indicated, or a specific prop. These things - physically identifiable elements demanded by the author - are given circumstances.

The script may also directly demand states-of-being, but these givens would not be considered circumstances. Again, circumstances refer to those things that could be identified as facts by an impartial observer.

The number of given circumstances can vary widely depending on the play or author. Some authors say very little directly, meaning the actor must do more work coming up with implied and imagined circumstances. Some authors have very strong visions of the characters already and may list such facts readily as they introduce characters and situations.

Implied Circumstances:

You may also be able to use the given information to make other inferences about the character. Maybe, for instance, the current scene happens in Alabama, and your character says they've never been anywhere else. Were they born in Alabama, then? Probably... but the script might not directly say so. Still, this is a fact that you can add to your list of circumstances and assume to be true, at least until something else comes along to contradict it.

Many useful character traits and life events may never be directly stated, such as a character's age, or family history, or occupation. But maybe there is enough there that you get a strong indication about something. If so, and especially if it is a factor that influences your character's inner life, then you should include it in your list of circumstances.

Imagined Circumstances:

A richly developed character, though, may have many attributes that were never stated in the script, nor even implied. Perhaps the script never mentions the parents of a character at all. Does this imply the character is an orphan? Hardly. It may be the case... Or it may not.

If there is no real way to know something about a character, an actor may choose in this case to specify the circumstances themselves. They may decide, for instance, that their father abandoned them as a child and their mother died when they were a teen. If these "facts" resonate with the actor in a way that makes the character seem more real, immediate, or authentic, then these imagined circumstances, made up entirely by the actor, should also be added to the list.

Imagined circumstances are the responsibility of the actor. Without these, a character may be flat, false, or merely a presentation of words and actions. When useful, character-defining traits are imagined by the actor the character's motivations become both more developed and more personally relevant to the actor.

Whether **given**, **implied**, or **imagined**, though, circumstances must refer to identifiable facts about the character, such as observable elements or definable events in their history. When a healthy, internally consistent list of such attributes has been created, it becomes much easier to do the further work of developing a character using Stanislavski's system.

Post Questions:

How is a "given circumstance" different from a "state of being?"

What is meant by "method acting?"

A circumstance that is completely made up by the actor is called:

Give two examples of “given circumstances” from your favorite story.

Why is it the responsibility of the actor to come up with imagined circumstances?

S H D Y B S C E N E K J D W V N T B O Z
N R E U C D W O O O A Z O Y M S R B V O
O E I V H I Q T N D Q A H T C C F H F N
I G L K D T T S U A L O T F A R D P K Y
T C P F T P T N X B D Y E B S I Q F X Y
C R M A G A T S E S U Q M A O P F A A U
E H I C N P S Y C H O L O G Y T N L B V
R L A T W J I D P E T T R J V A P C O S
I E I R K B E J F Q I U G C L Z M C R C
D N B F A N N L J J H A A Y F I O O A D
M O G C I C I K S V A L S I N A T S T H
G N M G H E T I W L W I R B R C I I N S
J E A I D A G E I T S H C V A Y V A H Y
G M P S X J R A R U P F B N L L A T A Q
I N P S E C N A T S M U C R I C T B J U
X X I M F J C M C S H L H I D D I U S Y
K P G T F H R M Q T M T D I B B O Y P X
G P I K C E H B Z T E R U E P U N Y L O
E B U I W A W X R W S R X Q U S J T C U
Y D Z W N O I T A N I G A M I O I I U A

Konstantin	script	character
Stanislavski	analysis	motivation
acting	circumstances	imagination
method	stage	authentic
actors	directions	implied
psychology	play	imagined
characters	scene